# Trust and Mercy

## The Heart of the Good News

by

Rev. George W. Kosicki, CSB

Published by

Franciscan University Press, Steubenville, Ohio
Marian Helpers, Stockbridge, Massachusetts
Divine Mercy Publications, Dublin, Ireland

## To all of us prodigal sons and daughters who so need God's Mercy

ACKNOWLEDGMENTS

My special thanks to those whose editorial help
has made this book available to you, the reader.

To:  Jim and Ann Sullivan
     Patricia Trahanas
     Sister Isabel Bettwy
     Sharon Montgomery

May the Merciful Lord bless
them with His peace and joy!

Scripture quotations are from the Greek translation, with
reference to various English translations, especially the
*Revised Standard Version*, the *New American Bible*, and the
*New American Bible with the Revised New Testament*.

Cover Art: H. Pinard and T. Bumgartner
Cover Design: Daniel F. Gallio

Published by:
Franciscan University Press, Steubenville, Ohio 43952
Marian Helpers, Stockbridge, Massachusetts 01263
Divine Mercy Publications, P.O. Box 2005, Dublin 13, Ireland

ISBN 0–940535–60–2

# CONTENTS

# INTRODUCTION

"She rediscovered the Gospel itself, the very heart of the Gospel." This astonishing statement was made by Pope Pius XII in his message of July 11, 1954, speaking of Saint Therese of Lisieux. It is an astonishing statement and implies something was lost and Saint Therese found it!

What was lost? What was found? Saint Therese found the resolution to the lost relationship of faith and works. Her life and teaching stressed that *the* work of God, the good work, is our free-will abandonment to the merciful love of God. *Trust* in God's mercy is *the* work which brings us salvation. Saint Therese offered herself totally, as she was, without reserve, with all her weaknesses, sins, and psychological anxieties, to the merciful love of God. She knew that she could not make it on her own. Her resolution was to plunge into the infinite ocean of God's mercy. These reflections on Saint Therese are developed by Madeleine F. Stebbins in *St. Therese of Lisieux: Doctor of the Church?* (New Rochelle, New York: C.U.F., 1992).

Saint Therese also found the treasure of spiritual childhood. We are to be little children in the arms of God, our Father. God's merciful love is available for all who trust Him. Her life teaches us that the simple daily duties of life, done in love, are the stuff of which sanctity is made.

*Trust and Mercy: The Heart of the Good News* is what Saint Therese rediscovered.

Trust and mercy comprise the heart of the Divine Mercy message and devotion as recorded for us by Blessed Faustina Kowalska. "What a dream team—Saint Therese and [Blessed] Faustina!" was how Fr. Harold Cohen, S.J., described them at the Divine Mercy Conference held at Franciscan University of Steubenville, Ohio, in July 1992.

Blessed Faustina had a special devotion to Saint Therese. It was Saint Therese who helped Blessed Faustina during her novitiate when she had a problem which she couldn't resolve. On the fifth day of a novena, Saint Therese appeared to Blessed Faustina in a dream, encouraging her to *"trust more in God"* and all would be resolved. Saint Therese also told Blessed Faustina that she would be a canonized saint someday. And "three days later the difficulty was solved very easily, just as she had said. And everything in this affair turned out exactly as she said it would. It was a dream, but it had its significance" (*Divine Mercy in My Soul: The Diary of the Servant of God Sister M. Faustina Kowalska* [Stockbridge, Massachusetts: Marian Helpers, 1987], p. 150).

*TRUST MORE!* That is the key issue in the lives of both Saint Therese and Blessed Faustina. This was the word I heard in my heart as I prayed at the tomb of Blessed Faustina in Lagiewniki, outside of Krakow, Poland: "I am your sister; trust the Lord even more."

*Trust the Lord even more!* summarizes the Pilgrimage to the Shrines of Divine Mercy in Poland and Vilnius which I made from September 15–28, 1992, with the Merciful Mother Association. And it is a word that continues to echo to this day in my heart.

Reflecting on the words of Pope Pius XII and the lives of Saint Therese and Blessed Faustina, I found new life in the words on faith and the work of God in the Gospel According to John. "This is the word of God: have faith in the one he sent" (John 6:29).

This "faith in the one he sent" is not just an acknowledgment of the truths of our creed, but it is faith in the person Jesus Christ, Son of God and Lord. It is *trust* in Jesus. *The* work of God is trust in God. Jesus called for trust: "Do not let your hearts be troubled. Have faith in God and have faith in me" (John 14:1). And Jesus continues: "I solemnly assure you, the man who has faith in me will do the works I do, and greater than these" (John 14:12).

Saint John then tells us the commandment of the Lord. It is a single commandment with two parts. His commandment is this: "We are to believe in the name of his Son, Jesus Christ, and we are to love one another as he commanded us" (1 John 3:23).

This is the twofold command of trust and mercy that was lived out by Saint Therese and Blessed Faustina. Trust and mercy are truly the heart of the Gospel because trust in the Lord Jesus opens the floodgates of His Merciful Heart. By trust we receive God's mercy, which makes it possible for us to be merciful even as our Father is merciful, and to love one another as we have been commanded.

And what is this trust? How did Saint Therese live it out in her life? She suffered from our modern-day problems of psychological anxieties. She went through a period of scruples, a time of hypersensitivity and even a nervous breakdown. She didn't wait until she was healed before she turned to the Lord. She went as she was, with her knapsack full of emotional problems, and plunged with complete trust into the loving mercy of God. She made an oblation of her life to Merciful Love.

Blessed Faustina lived out trust by offering herself to the Lord's mercy so that she would be transformed into

3

mercy (cf. *Diary*, 163). She would hide in the Merciful Heart of Jesus as a refuge and strength. Blessed Faustina would plunge herself into the infinite ocean of God's mercy and be enveloped by His mercy (cf. *Diary*, 1572, 1777).

> When I see that the burden is beyond my strength, I do not consider or analyze it or probe into it, but I run like a child to the Heart of Jesus and say only one word to Him: "You can do all things." And then I keep silent.... [*Diary*, 1033; see also 1621, 1629.]

Trust is a total reliance upon the saving truth that Jesus Christ is Mercy itself. Trust is a walk of faith and hope in Jesus. It is a walk with Jesus, not knowing the answers, not feeling His presence, not having all in control or in order. Trust is the great act of our free will by which we place our confidence in the Merciful Savior.

Trust is what Mary, the Mother of Jesus, was blessed for by her cousin Elizabeth: "Blest is she who trusted that the Lord's word would be fulfilled" (Luke 1:45).

Mary expressed her trust in the answer she gave to the Angel, "Let it be done to me according to your word" (Luke 1:38).

Pope John Paul II in his encyclical on Divine Mercy, *Dives in Misericordia*, describes how Christ demands from us a life of trust and mercy, by being guided by love and mercy:

> Christ, in revealing the love, mercy of God, at the same time *demanded from the people* that they also be guided in their lives by love and mercy. This demand forms the very essence of the messianic proclamation, and the very essence of the Gospel's distinguishing character [*ethos*]. [George W. Kosicki, C.S.B., trans., *Dives in Misericordia*, n. 3.]

4

The "heart of the Gospel" calls us to be "guided by love and mercy," to *trust* in God's mercy and to receive His mercy, which is the first act of trust. The Holy Father points out that Christ expressed this demand of mercy as "the greatest commandment" and also "in the form of a blessing, when in the Sermon on the Mount, He proclaims: 'Blessed are the merciful, for they shall obtain mercy'" (ibid., n. 3; Matt 5:7; 22:38).

To trust in God's mercy is the heart of the Gospel. It is the rediscovery of Saint Therese's message of spiritual childhood and it is also the message of the revelations to Blessed Faustina. It is capsulized in the prayer given to Blessed Faustina which she was told by Jesus to inscribe at the bottom of the image of the Merciful Savior: *Jesus, I trust in You!*

Jesus, who is Mercy itself, is the object of our free act of trust. As we place all our trust in Him, we are filled with His mercy which makes it possible for us to be merciful. By trusting in Jesus, we fulfill His twofold command to believe in Him and to love one another (cf. 1 John 3:23).

By trust and mercy, we live the heart of the Gospel.

# OVERVIEW

This book, *Trust and Mercy: The Heart of the Good News*, is an attempt to show the centrality and importance of the message and devotion of Divine Mercy. This devotion is not just a private devotion of personal choice. Rather, it is God's devotion for you and me. Mercy is of the very nature of God. He is love, and that love poured out in creating, redeeming, and sanctifying us, *is* mercy.

This book is divided into four parts. Part One is a reflection on the relationship of God and man. God's part is to be merciful. Our part is to trust in Him, to receive His mercy, and to be merciful to others as our heavenly Father is merciful.

Part Two looks into the Sacred Scriptures to see how mercy is at the heart of both the Old and the New Testaments. A survey of texts on mercy shows how mercy is the heart of Gospels and Epistles. The fullness of the revelation of Divine Mercy is in the pierced Heart of Jesus on the Cross. This is shown by the early Fathers' use of Sacred Scripture and by private revelation approved by all the popes of this past century.

Part Three deals with our need to be totally immersed in God's mercy, or to use the Greek word for immersion, baptized in His mercy, and then to live baptized in His mercy.

Part Four reflects on the goal and mission of mercy, which is to make the Father's mercy present. In the Mystical Body of Christ we are to be mercy, to be Eucharist, and to be Mary. This is the new wave of the Holy Spirit: Mercy, Mary, and Eucharist.

# PART ONE

# MERCY, GOD, AND MAN

# 1

## Why Don't We Get Together?

ON THE ONE HAND, we are told that God is Mercy itself and wants to have mercy on all. But on the other hand, we know for a fact that we are miserable sinners in need of mercy. So, why don't we get together? The word of God tells us that God is love (cf. 1 John 4:16), and that love poured out in creating us, redeeming us, and sanctifying us is mercy. Mercy is love's second name according to Pope John Paul II (cf. *Dives in Misericordia*). God so loved us that He gave His only Son that we might have a new and eternal life (cf. John 3:16). God's great plan of love is to have mercy on all (cf. Rom 11:32). He stands at the door of our hearts and knocks, waiting for us to open our hearts to Him so that He might dine with us and give us the throne of victory (cf. Rev 3:19-22).

God stands at the door of our hearts and waits. Herein lies the revealing clue, the reason why we don't get together. God *waits* for our free invitation to enter our lives. He waits for our freely given "yes," our free "come," our "welcome." Our freedom is the issue. God created us with a free will and He wants us to exercise our freedom by asking for His mercy. He will not violate that freedom which He created us with by forcing His mercy upon us, even though it is His greatest desire that we receive His mercy. And so God waits for us, His creatures, to accept freely His mercy. What a humble God who waits upon us in such love!

The tragic part of this "waiting" is that God's mercy is infinite and available, and that human beings are in such desperate need of it! Yet we do not turn to His mercy with trust. How pointedly the mystic, Blessed Faustina, writes of Our Lord's promises to those in need of His mercy:

Even if the sins of souls will be as dark as night, when the sinner turns to My mercy he gives Me the greatest praise. [*Diary*, 378.]

[Let] the greatest sinners place their trust in My mercy. They have the right before others to trust in the abyss of My mercy. [*Diary*, 1146.]

The greater the misery of a soul, the greater its right to My mercy. [*Diary*, 1182.]

I am more generous toward sinners than toward the just. [*Diary*, 1275.]

Oh, if sinners knew My mercy, they would not perish in such great numbers. [*Diary*, 1396.]

We are sinners and we are miserable! Consider the sins we need to repent of in order to receive God's mercy:

· Sins of *commission:* breaking the Ten Commandments and committing the seven capital sins of anger, lust, intemperance, sloth, avarice, envy, and pride.

· Sins of *omission:* not loving one another as Christ loves us, not being merciful as our heavenly Father; not forgiving one another.

· Sins of *waste:* wasting graces, wasting talents, and wasting time. Yes, even wasting our sufferings! Suffering is the way the Father chose for Jesus to reveal His mercy. Suffering is a precious channel of mercy to others.

And what about our idols?

· Sins of *idolatry:* making idols of our success and repu-
tation, and making idols of our values, attitudes, and
possessions.

· And to top off our sins of idolatry, self-centeredness,
*pride.*

· Sins of *self-salvation:* trying to merit God's mercy by
our own effort; trying to save just ourselves and not being
concerned for others, living just for ourselves without a
concern for God.

In addition to our personal sins we suffer the effects of
social sins. My sin affects you; your sin affects me. There
is a solidarity in sin that makes us *miserable.* Our misery
expresses itself in a number of ways: boredom, frustra-
tion, depression, anger, lack of forgiveness, fears,
confusion, sickness, violence, abuse, jealousies, divisions.
The list goes on and on. This solidarity in sin is experienced by the mass of mankind in a variety of injustices,
poverty of material, spiritual, cultural and emotional
needs, wars, and tragedies. In a word, MISERY.

There is no doubt that we are sinners and that we are
miserable. We need mercy. The only answer to the di-
lemma of the world is God's mercy. No humor program
is adequate to respond to our desperate need of mercy.
We must turn to God's mercy with trust as the only source
of peace (cf. *Diary*, 300).

When we receive God's mercy we become channels of
His mercy to others, bearers of peace. The miserable world
situation has infected the Church with a secularization
that is like a malignant cancer. Consider some of the signs
of secularization within the Church: a plurality of

personal infallibility, selective obedience, and demo-cratization of faith. Is this secularization the reason for the loss and decrease of vocations of priests and religious, for the decrease in missionary evangelization?

We all need God's mercy.

# 2

## How Do We Connect up with God's Mercy?

THE CONNECTION with God's mercy depends on us. We need to make a free act of our will. God for His part is always ready and willing to fill us with His mercy if we freely open ourselves to Him. Our part in the connection can be described with three R's: Repent, Receive, and Respond. These three actions of our free will are related and overlap since one leads to the other.

*Repent:* Turning away from our sin and our self-centeredness and turning toward the merciful God, we acknowledge and admit our guilt and need for mercy. Repentance is a resolution to change our way of life by means of God's grace and mercy. It can be thought of as an emptying of ourselves of all that is not of God in order to be filled with His mercy.

As Catholics we have the tremendous gift of the Sacrament of Reconciliation. We come to Christ's representative in the "Tribunal of Mercy," as our Lord described it to Blessed Faustina, in order to receive mercy, not a sentence of condemnation. We don't make a grocery list for its own sake, but in order to buy groceries, to bring them home, and to prepare a meal to eat, so that we may be nourished. The purpose of the Sacrament is not to make a grocery list of sins, but rather to bring to the Father our need for mercy and then to receive His mercy.

The prayer of absolution the priest says over the penitent describes God's mercy in the redemption won for us by Jesus and given to us by the Holy Spirit. Each phrase is a prayer for mercy:

> God, the Father of mercies, / through the death and resurrection of his Son / has reconciled the world to himself / and sent the Holy Spirit among us / for the forgiveness of sins; / through the ministry of the Church / may God give you pardon and peace, / and I absolve you from your sins, / in the name of the Father, and of the Son, / and of the Holy Spirit. / Amen.

Repenting of sin is something we need to do repeatedly; it is not just a single event. Repenting can be compared to turning the steering wheel of the car to keep it on the road. We continuously need to adjust our direction to focus on the Lord and keep our eyes on Jesus. We need to repent (cf. Heb 12:2).

Thanks be to God that He never tires of our repentance. He tells us through Blessed Faustina that His greatest sorrow is the loss of souls, souls who do not repent (cf. *Diary*, 1397). In fact, what is even worse than the sin we commit is our not turning to God's mercy after we have sinned because it means we are refusing His mercy.

To repent means to *ask* for His mercy. Asking makes all the difference in the world. Adam and Eve never asked for mercy after they sinned. But King David, the chosen and beloved of God, after being confronted by the prophet Nathan for committing adultery and murder, pleaded for mercy: Have mercy on me, a sinner! (cf. Psalm 51). God answered his plea for mercy and chose him as the ancestor of Christ. What a different world we would have if Adam and Eve had cried out, "We have sinned. Have mercy on us in Your great mercy!"

*Receive:* How important it is to receive God's mercy! It is only by His mercy that we are forgiven, cleansed, and redeemed. It is only by His mercy that we can be merciful to others in need, merciful even as our heavenly Father is merciful (cf. Luke 6:36).

To receive God's mercy, we need not only to repent, but we also need to trust in God. Trust is the total reliance upon saving truth, upon Jesus Christ. Trust is an act of free will. It is at the same time an act of faith, of hope, and of love. Trust is the key that opens the Merciful Heart of Jesus, the key that opens the floodgates of mercy.

Trust is the fundamental act of the will by which we receive mercy. Jesus asked Blessed Faustina to have His image signed, "Jesus, I trust in You!" When we sign the image, it is our part of the covenant of mercy, it is our consecration to the Merciful Savior. To those who trust in Him, He promises unimaginable graces (cf. *Diary*, 1146, 1578, 1739, 1777, 1784).

The Lord not only wants us to receive His mercy; He wants us to be immersed in it so it can overflow to others. He wants us baptized in His mercy.

*Respond:* The purpose of our receiving God's mercy is so that we will be merciful to others: by deed, by word, and by prayer (*Diary*, 742). The measure of our response is the command of the Lord, "Be merciful, just as your heavenly Father is merciful" (Luke 6:36).

The only possible way that we can be merciful as the Father is merciful is to receive *His* mercy and then give it away. We can't give what we don't have. But once we receive the Father's mercy we can respond with His own mercy and so fulfill the Lord's command to be merciful. By His mercy we can radiate mercy (cf. *Diary*, 1074).

Another way to describe what we can do to connect with God's mercy is in the "ABC's" of mercy:

**A**sk for His mercy (cf. Luke 11:9).
**B**e merciful and so obtain mercy (cf. Matt 5:7).
**C**ompletely trust in Jesus.

To ask, to be merciful, and to trust in Jesus are all acts of our free will. When we freely turn to the Merciful Savior in our need for mercy, He cannot resist.

# 3

## The Heart of It All

GOD'S MERCY is most fully revealed in the pierced Heart of His Son. Mercy is the heart of it all. The two hands of Jesus depicted in the image of the Merciful Savior (cf. *Diary*, 47-49) demonstrate this. His left hand points to the area of His Heart from which the blood and water gush forth as rays of mercy. Jesus points to the source of all mercy. He invites all of us who are sinful and miserable to come to His Merciful Heart: "Come to me all you who are weary and burdened. . ." (Matt 11:28). His right hand is raised in priestly blessing, bestowing peace, the Spirit, and forgiveness: in a word, MERCY.

Mercy is the heart of the Gospel. Mercy summarizes the first preaching of Jesus (cf. Mark 1:15) and culminates on the Cross in the greatest sacrifice of mercy. The victory of resurrection is shared in the Easter Sunday night appearance of Jesus when He bestowed His mercy (cf. John 20:19-23).

According to Pope John Paul II, mercy is most fully revealed in the Heart of Jesus pierced for us on the Cross (cf. *Dives in Misericordia*, n. 13) and extended to us through the maternal heart of Mary (ibid., n. 9; *Redemptor Hominis*, n. 22).

The heart of the mission of Jesus is to *make mercy present* (cf. *Dives in Misericordia, Redemptoris Missio*). This, then, is the mission of the Church and our mission: to make mercy present.

The final goal of the mission of mercy is the union of hearts, our heart with the Heart of Jesus. It is a union of love and a total, humble, obedient surrender to the will of the Father. Mary, whose Immaculate Heart is united with the Merciful Heart of her Son, is the model and mother of our final goal. She forms our hearts by the Spirit to be one with the Heart of her Son. So we can pray, "Mary, my mother, as you formed the Heart of Jesus by the Spirit, form my heart to be the throne of Jesus in His glorious coming."

And how fortunate we are to receive the mercy of Jesus through the heart of His mother. How fortunate we are that we don't have to be lovable to be loved. The qualification to receive mercy is that we are miserable! And how perfectly we qualify in our sinful misery! We really do need a heart transplant and we don't have to wait for a donor. Jesus has already donated His Heart, ready to transform our hearts. In the Litany of the Sacred Heart of Jesus, we pray, "Jesus, meek and humble of Heart, make our hearts like unto Thine."

Yes, mercy is the heart of the Gospel, because "the heart of mercy is love" (*Dives in Misericordia*) writes John Seward in his study of Saint Thomas Aquinas on mercy, "Love's Second Name" (*The Canadian Catholic Review*, March 1990). Seward draws on the treasures of Scripture, Aristotle, Augustine, Shakespeare, Hans Urs von Balthasar, and John Paul II to present a rich theology of mercy. Saint Thomas' definition of mercy remains with me. He describes mercy in the Latin word *misericordia* (cf. *Summa Theologica*, II-II.30.1), meaning "having a miserable heart." He points out two aspects of mercy: first, the affective aspect which feels the plight of another, and second, the effective aspect which takes positive action to relieve that pain. In present day language I would translate Saint Thomas to say that "mercy is to have a pain in our hearts over the pain of another and to take pains to relieve that pain."

Yes, mercy is the heart of it all.

# PART TWO

# MERCY: THE HEART
# OF SACRED SCRIPTURE

# 4

## Mercy: The Heart of the Old Testament

IN HIS *DICTIONARY OF THE BIBLE,* John L. McKenzie concludes the description of mercy in the Old Testament as the "heart" from which mercy flows. "The word [mercy] indicates a broad and embracing benevolence, a will to do good to another rather than evil. It is not precisely love or kindness but the goodness of the heart from which love and kindness arise."

McKenzie begins his article by pointing out that the Hebrew word *hesed* has no adequate translation. We use "mercy" in English. Scholars agree that the divine and human attitude designated by *hesed* is basic to Hebrew religion and morality. The author states that the meaning of *hesed* is seen most clearly in the words associated with it. *Hesed* is *emet* (faithfulness), *mispat* (judgment), *sedakah* (righteousness), *yeshua* (salvation), *rahamim* (tenderness), *berit* (covenant). The most frequently associated word is *berit,* which came to be expressed in the bond of the covenant with God.

According to McKenzie, "The entire history of the dealing of Yahweh with Israel can be summed up as *hesed.*" *Hesed* is the key to understanding Yahweh's character.

Francis L. Anderson in a study of the texts in the Old Testament using *hesed* (cf. "Yahweh, the Kind and

23

Sensitive God" in *God Who is Rich in Mercy* (Peter T. O'Brien and David G. Peterson, editors [Australia: Lancer Books, 1986]), says that trying to define *hesed* is like trying to define God. "The heart of the matter," he explains, "is a generous and beneficial action, not at all required" (p. 44). In examining all two hundred and fifty texts where *hesed* occurs he cites Exodus 34:6-7 as the most sublime and most complete of those related statements. It stands absolute as the Lord's own self-declaration, "Yahweh, Yahweh, / compassionate and gracious God, / Slow to anger and abundant in *hesed* and *emet*" (p. 46).

Other closely related texts—Deuteronomy 5:9-10, Exodus 20:5-6, Numbers 14:18-19, and Deuteronomy 7:9-12—are "variations on the same theme." Anderson points out that *hesed* is the foundation of God's dealings with humans; it is pure generosity from God's side. The Lord maintains *hesed* as love and blessing, not as a reward or payment. He does it on the grounds of His own promise, not on the basis of man's righteous conduct. *Hesed* has no cause outside God Himself. *Hesed* as love in action is seen in the biblical stories of Abraham, Moses, Joshua, David, and the prophets.

From the Anderson study it is clear "that doing *hesed* is the supreme attribute of God, so that a person is most like God when he does *hesed*" (p. 72) (e.g., Jer 9:23; 32:18; 33:11; Hos 2:21; 4:1; 6:4, 6).

Anderson groups his study of the 141 times the word *hesed* appears in the Psalms, Job, and Proverbs and explains that *hesed* is an object of trust and hope; the ground of appeal in prayer; the basis of God's repentance; the means of salvation; the basis for forgiveness; the object of praise; often associated with other attributes such as justice and compassion; eternal and limitless in scope (cf. p. 80).

Anderson concludes his study with a five-point summary:

1. In the old biblical stories *"hesed* mainly describes exceptional acts of one human to another."

2. "The earliest revelations of God's character . . . highlight his *hesed* as primal, enduring, and associated with his love, grace, compassion, rather than with justice."

3. "The prophets associate *hesed* with a cluster of virtues . . . giving it more associations with justice."

4. "In the Psalms, *hesed* is the supreme attribute of God, associated with both justice and compassion."

5. "In later writings . . . *hesed* comes to denote piety in general. . . ." [Pp. 81–82.]

This study of *hesed* in the Old Testament, which is confirmed and strengthened by the reflections of Pope John Paul II, illustrates the centrality of God's mercy in the life of the people of Israel. "The people of God of the Old Covenant had drawn from their age-long history a special experience of the mercy of God. . . ."

In the preaching of the prophets, *mercy signifies a special power of love,* which *prevails over the sin and infidelity* of the Chosen People. . . .

. . . All the subtleties of love become manifest in the Lord's mercy toward those who are His own; He is their Father (cf. Isa 63:16), for Israel is His firstborn son (cf. Exod 4:22). The Lord is also the bridegroom of her whose name the prophet proclaims: *Ruhamah,* "Beloved" or "she has obtained pity" (cf. Hos 2:3). . . .

... Love, so to speak, conditions justice and, in the final analysis, justice serves love. The primacy and superiority of love in the face of justice—and this is the mark of the whole of revelation—*are revealed precisely through mercy.* [*Dives in Misericordia*, n. 4.]

In the chapter on the "Mercy of God in the Mission of the Church," John Paul further confirms and develops the meaning of *hesed:*

If some theologians claim that mercy is the greatest of the attributes and perfections of God, then to this the Bible, Tradition and the whole faith life of the People of God provide unique proof. . . .

*The Church* lives an authentic life when she *professes and proclaims* the most stupendous attribute of the Creator and Redeemer and when she brings people close to the sources of the Savior's *mercy.* [Ibid., n. 13.]

Mercy is the heart of the Old Testament and the New Testament because God is not only a God of mercy but is Mercy itself. He is *the* Divine Mercy. The description of God as Divine Mercy is most clearly and beautifully recorded in the diary of Blessed Faustina, the "Apostle of Divine Mercy." The next chapter in this book is an excerpt from my book *Special Urgency of Mercy: Why Sister Faustina?*, and gives a summary of Our Lord's description of His Mercy, for He says, "I am Mercy itself" (*Diary*, 281, 300, 1074, 1148, 1273, 1739, 1777).

The following mnemonic using the word "mercy" is a helpful way to remember who this Divine Mercy is:

**M**ighty
**E**ternal
**R**edeemer
**C**ompassionate
**Y**ahweh

And "'God who is rich in mercy' (Eph 2:4) is the one whom Jesus Christ revealed to us as *Father*. It is His very own Son who revealed Him and made Him visible in Himself" (*Dives in Misericordia*, n. 1).

"The invisible God *becomes visible in Christ and through Christ*," who "*incarnates mercy and personifies it. In a sense, Christ Himself is mercy*" (ibid., n. 2).

# 5

## How Does God Describe His Mercy?

THIS CHAPTER is adapted from *Special Urgency of Mercy: Why Sister Faustina?* (Steubenville, Ohio: Franciscan University Press; Stockbridge, Massachusetts: Marian Helpers; Dublin, Ireland: Divine Mercy Publications, 1990).

"I am Mercy itself" (*Diary*, 281, 300, 1074, 1148, 1273, 1739, 1777) is how God describes His mercy to Blessed Faustina. Saint John tells us that "God is love" (1 John 4:16). The two descriptions complement each other. God in Himself is love and when that love is poured out in creation, redemption, and sanctification, it is mercy. Mercy is God's love poured out. It is love's second name (cf. John Paul II, *Dives in Misericordia*). The Lord delights in the title "Mercy" (*Diary*, 300) because it so beautifully describes who He is and how He longs to pour out His mercy on us. He also calls Himself the "King of Mercy" (*Diary*, 83, 88), and the "Merciful Savior" (*Diary*, 1075, 1541), and He refers to His "Merciful Heart" (e.g., *Diary*, 177, 1074, 1152, 1447, 1520, 1588, 1602, 1682, 1689, 1728, 1739, 1777). But those titles give only a hint of His great desire to be merciful.

Throughout her diary, Blessed Faustina records for us the words of the Lord describing the great desire He has to share His mercy with souls. He yearns for souls (cf. *Diary*, 206, 1182, 1521, 1784) and He keeps pouring out His mercy (cf. *Diary*, 50, 177, 699, 703, 1074, 1159, 1190, 1689, 1784), clamoring to be spent (cf. *Diary*, 177) like a burning flame within Him (cf. *Diary*, 50, 177, 186, 1074, 1190, 1521). His desire is greatest for sinners (cf. *Diary*, 206, 378, 723, 1146, 1275, 1665, 1739, 1541). His compassion overflows (cf. *Diary*, 1148, 1190, 1777) with arms open and waiting (cf. *Diary*, 206, 1541, 1728, 1777). He excludes no one (cf. *Diary*, 1076, 1182, 1728), and asks only for trust, unlimited trust. His mercy defends us (cf. *Diary*, 1516), especially at the hour of death (cf. *Diary*, 378, 379, 754, 1075, 1540). But the description of His mercy on us is not enough; there is more.

The Lord also describes the very nature of His mercy, but there is no adequate language for it. It is ineffable (cf. *Diary*, 359) and cannot be imagined or conceived with our minds (cf. *Diary*, 699, 1142). So the Lord uses a variety of adjectives and images to give us some appreciation of the magnificence of His mercy. He compares it to an ocean (cf. *Diary*, 699, 718, 1209, 1210, 1214, 1216, 1218, 1273, 1520) with bottomless depth (cf. *Diary*, 88, 420, 570, 699, 811, 848, 1059, 1142, 1146, 1182, 1190, 1517, 1777) with no limits and inexhaustible (cf. *Diary*, 50, 718, 1273) like a great abyss (cf. *Diary*, 180, 206, 1226, 1228, 1541, 1576, 1777). It is infinite (cf. *Diary*, 378, 687, 689); it is great (cf. *Diary*, 300, 378, 379, 635, 699, 965, 1396).

The Lord also uses the image of a fountain echoing the image of John's Gospel: "Let anyone who thirsts come to me and drink. . . . Rivers of living water will flow from within him" (John 7:37-38). This fount of mercy (cf. *Diary*, 187, 327, 848, 1075, 1182, 1209, 1488, 1520, 1602, 1777) is opened wide for us (cf. *Diary*, 1146, 1159, 1182, 1520, 1572).

In a wonderful way, the Lord describes His pierced side from which gushed forth blood and water as a fount of mercy (cf. *Diary*, 187). The great mercy of our Lord is like an ocean and like a fountain, and yet it is tender (cf. *Diary*, 420, 699, 811, 848). It is the greatest of His attributes (cf. *Diary*, 180, 301). Mercy is His love poured out on us. It is confirmed in every work, culminating in forgiveness (cf. *Diary*, 723).

The Lord portrayed His mercy visually to Blessed Faustina as rays of red and pale light coming from His pierced side, as rays from the fount of mercy (cf. *Diary*, 1309). These rays of His merciful love (cf. *Diary*, 370) issued from the very depths of His tender mercy when His agonizing Heart was opened with a lance on the Cross (cf. *Diary*, 299). Not only did Blessed Faustina see these rays of mercy from the area of the Heart of Jesus as depicted in the image of the Merciful Savior, but on a number of occasions she saw these same two rays emanating from the Eucharist (cf. *Diary*, 336, 344, 370, 420, 441, 657, 1046) and from His Sacred Heart (cf. *Diary*, 177, 414, 1559, 1565, 1796). At times she saw the rays covering the whole world (cf. *Diary*, 87, 441, 1796).

Jesus exhorts us to live in the shelter of these rays of mercy shielded from the just hand of God and His wrath (cf. *Diary*, 299). Is it any wonder that God's mercy is praised by the souls in heaven (cf. *Diary*, 753)?

> Oh, the depth of the riches and wisdom and the knowledge of God! How inscrutable are his judgments and how unsearchable his ways!...For from him and through him and for him are all things. To him be glory forever. Amen. [Rom 11:30-36.]

As an example of the description of God's mercy and His great desire for the souls of sinners, the dialogue of the merciful God with a sinful soul stands out as a prime example:

**Jesus:** Be not afraid of your Savior, O sinful soul. I make the first move to come to you, for I know that by yourself you are unable to lift yourself to Me. Child, do not run away from your Father; be willing to talk openly with your God of mercy who wants to speak words of pardon and lavish His graces on you. How dear your soul is to Me! I have inscribed your name upon My hand; you are engraved as a deep wound in My Heart.

**Soul:** Lord, I hear Your voice calling me to turn back from the path of sin, but I have neither the strength nor the courage to do so.

**Jesus:** I am your strength, I will help you in the struggle.

**Soul:** Lord, I recognize Your holiness, and I fear You.

**Jesus:** My child, do you fear the God of mercy? My holiness does not prevent Me from being merciful. Behold, for you I have established a throne of mercy on earth—the tabernacle—and from this throne I desire to enter into your heart. I am not surrounded by a retinue or guards. You can come to Me at any moment, at any time; I want to speak to you and desire to grant you grace.

**Soul:** Lord, I doubt that You will pardon my numerous sins; my misery fills me with fright.

**Jesus:** My mercy is greater than your sins and those of the entire world. Who can measure the extent of My goodness? For you I descended from heaven to earth; for you I allowed Myself to be nailed to the cross; for you I let My Sacred Heart be pierced with a lance, thus opening wide the source of mercy for you. Come, then, with trust to draw graces from this fountain. I never reject a contrite heart. Your misery has disappeared in the depths of My mercy. Do not argue with Me about your wretchedness. You will give Me pleasure if you hand over to Me all your troubles and griefs. I shall heap upon you the treasures of My grace.

**Soul:** You have conquered, O Lord, my stony heart with Your goodness. In trust and humility I approach the tribunal of Your mercy, where You Yourself absolve me by the hand of Your representative. O Lord, I feel Your grace and Your peace filling my poor soul. I feel overwhelmed by Your mercy, O Lord. You forgive me, which is more than I dared to hope for or could imagine. Your goodness surpasses all my desires. And now, filled with gratitude for so many graces, I invite You to my heart. I wandered, like a prodigal child gone astray; but You did not cease to be my Father. Increase Your mercy toward me, for You see how weak I am.

**Jesus:** Child, speak no more of your misery; it is already forgotten. Listen, My child, to what I desire to tell you. Come close to My wounds and draw from the fountain of Life whatever your heart desires. Drink copiously from the fountain of Life and you will not weary on your journey. Look at the splendors of My mercy and do not fear the enemies of your salvation. Glorify My mercy. [*Diary*, 1485.]

The conversations of the merciful God with a despairing soul (cf. *Diary*, 1486), with a suffering soul (cf. *Diary*, 1487), with a soul striving after perfection (cf. *Diary*, 1488), and with a perfect soul (cf. *Diary*, 1489) are a marvelous set of teachings on God's mercy. They are printed as a pamphlet on the interior life and can be used for frequent reading and reflection by all of us (Marian Helpers, 1993).

# 6

## The Heart of the Gospel Is Mercy

THE HEART OF THE GOSPEL is mercy come in person. Jesus Christ *"incarnates mercy and personifies it"* says Pope John Paul II (*Dives in Misericordia*, n. 2).

In the New Testament, *hesed* (mercy, loving kindness) carries all the rich meaning of the Old Testament with the added dimension of "readiness to forgive" our sins. Saint Paul puts it very directly: "Through him [Christ] we have redemption, the forgiveness of our sins" (Col 1:14).

The beginning, middle, and end of the life, message, and mission of Jesus is mercy: mercy proclaimed, demonstrated, poured out, and commissioned. It is important for us to see that the heart of the mission of Jesus was to make the mercy of the Father present. It is the very mission of the Church and the mission of each one of us to do the same: to make the mercy of the Father present. A sketch of the Gospel will help to show the centrality of the mission of mercy.

MERCY IN THE BEGINNING OF THE GOSPEL

Jesus begins his public life by proclaiming the Kingdom of God and calls for our response of repentance and trust (cf. Mark 1:15). Each phrase is a call to mercy:

"The time is fulfilled," now is the time for mercy.

"The kingdom of God is at hand," mercy is present and available.

"Repent," turn from sin and self and receive mercy.

"And believe," trust, living faith is the key to mercy.

"In the gospel," Jesus, Mercy Incarnate, is the Gospel, the Good News.

In the opening words of the encyclical *Dives in Misericordia*, we hear the same summary of the mission of Jesus: "'God who is rich in mercy' is the one whom Jesus Christ revealed to us as *Father*. It is His very own Son who revealed Him and made Him visible in Himself" (n. 1).

Saint Matthew describes the beginning of Jesus's public mission succinctly. Jesus began immediately to preach, "Repent, for the kingdom of heaven is at hand" (Matt 4:17).

Saint Luke, using the words of Isaiah the prophet, describes the beginning of the mission of Jesus as the announcement of the Gospel of Mercy to those in misery:

> The Spirit of the Lord is upon me, because he has anointed me to preach good news to the poor. He has sent me to proclaim release to the captives and recovery of sight to the blind, to set at liberty those who are oppressed, to proclaim the acceptable year of the Lord. [Luke 4:18-19.]

The Gospel According to Luke is known as the Gospel of Mercy. How beautifully the prophet Zechariah proclaims that "through the tender mercy of God,... day shall dawn upon us from on high" (Luke 1:78). In her Magnificat Mary says:

> And his mercy is on those who fear him
>    from generation to generation. . . .

He has helped his servant Israel,
in remembrance of his mercy. . . .

[Luke 1:50, 54-55.]

## Mercy in the Middle of the Gospel

The example of Jesus' compassion, His teachings and parables, as well as His miracles, all proclaim mercy and make it present to those in misery.

Saint Mark records for us how Jesus pitied the vast crowd, for they were like sheep without a shepherd (cf. Mark 6:34, 8:2). He taught them at great length and fed the thousands by multiplying bread and fish (cf. Mark 6:35-44, 8:1-9). "Moved with pity," Jesus cured the leper (cf. Mark 1:40-45). Seeing the faith of the men carrying the paralyzed man, He forgave sins (cf. Mark 2:5). He embraced children and blessed them (cf. Mark 10:14-16).

Saint Matthew in the Sermon on the Mount describes in the Beatitudes God's mercy to the miserable, explicitly saying, "Blessed are the merciful, for they will be shown mercy" (Matt 5:7).

Further, Jesus commands love of our enemies and prayer for our persecutors (cf. Matt 5:43-48). The one phrase of the Our Father that Jesus comments on is that we forgive (cf. Matt 6:14-15) and that we be merciful.

Saint Matthew describes how Jesus tempers justice with mercy, thus fulfilling the words of the Prophet Isaiah:

> Behold my servant whom I have chosen, my beloved with whom my soul is well pleased. I will put my Spirit upon him, and he shall proclaim justice to the Gentiles. He will not wrangle or cry aloud, nor will anyone hear his voice in the streets; he will not break a bruised reed

or quench a smoldering wick, till he brings justice to victory; and in his name will the Gentiles hope.
[Isa 42:1-3; Matt 12:18-21.]

In the parable of the merciless official, Jesus calls us to mercy. "My heavenly Father will treat you in exactly the same way unless each of you forgives his brother from his heart" (Matt 18:35).

Jesus teaches us the greatest command of the law. This command of love is a command to be merciful.

You shall love the Lord, your God, with all your heart, and with all your soul, and with all your mind. This is the great and first commandment. And the second is like it, you shall love your neighbor as yourself. On these two commandments depend all the law and prophets.
[Matt 22:37-40.]

Saint Luke gives the great command of mercy as "Be merciful, even as your Father is merciful" (Luke 6:36).

Jesus showed this mercy in healing all who came to Him (cf. Luke 6:17-19). He taught the people to be merciful in the Beatitudes (cf. Matt 5:7). He forgave the sins of the penitent woman (cf. Luke 7:36-50), and He gave sight to a blind man who cried out for mercy (cf. Luke 18:35-43). He taught mercy in the great parables of mercy: the good Samaritan (cf. Luke 10:25-37); the lost sheep (cf. Luke 15:1-7); the lost coin (cf. Luke 15:8-10); and the lost prodigal son (cf. Luke 15:11-32). In the parable of the prodigal son we hear of the great mercy of the father who restores the sonship of the prodigal son. He restores the meaning, the value, and the dignity of the younger son. This is the greatest parable of God's mercy according to John Paul II (in *Dives in Misericordia*), even though the word "mercy" is not mentioned.

As Jesus begins the Last Supper, He speaks of His infinite love for His Apostles. He loved His own who were in the world and would show His love to the end (cf. John 13:1).

Jesus then reveals His mercy in the washing of the feet of His disciples, in the institution of the Holy Eucharist, and in the great discourse of loving mercy (cf. John 13-17; Luke 22:14–20).

But the fullness of His mercy is revealed in His passion, death, and resurrection as is recorded for us by the four Evangelists. Pope John Paul II, in the chapter the "Paschal Mystery" in *Dives in Misericordia*, says that the paschal mystery is the culmination of the radical revelation of mercy, and that the paschal Christ is the definitive incarnation of mercy. In the chapter "The Mercy of God in the Mission of the Church," he says that the Heart of Jesus reveals the merciful love of the Father, "a revelation which makes up the central content of the messianic mission of the Son of God" (n. 13).

The Heart of Jesus reveals the heart of the Gospel!

On Easter Sunday night Jesus reveals His mercy and bestows it on His Apostles. He comes through the locked door of the upper room and says "Peace," *"Shalom,"* the fullness of all blessings, mercy. He shows His hands and His pierced side, the source of all mercy. Again, He says, *"Shalom."* He breathes on them the Holy Spirit, the Spirit of loving mercy itself. And, as He commissions them with the same mission He received from the Father, to make mercy present, He bestows the power of merciful love, forgiveness. Jesus empowers the Church to forgive sin, the great work of mercy, our redemption (cf. Col 1:14). Jesus makes His Apostles "ambassadors of reconciliation" (2 Cor 5:17-21).

From beginning, through the middle, and to the end of the Gospel, mercy is present in the person of Jesus—visible, tangible, and believable. The Merciful Heart of Jesus is the heart of the Gospel.

"Come to me, all you who are weary and find life burdensome, and I will refresh you. Take my yoke upon your shoulders and learn from me, for I am gentle and humble of heart. Your souls will find rest, for my yoke is easy and my burden light" (Matt 11:28-30).

# 7

## Mercy in the Epistles

THE MERCY OF GOD is portrayed with a special richness in the Epistles. It is by God's mercy that we are forgiven and reconciled, and by His mercy we receive salvation. A survey of some of the texts that use the word mercy and related words such as love and kindness, as well as the fruits of mercy, forgiveness and reconciliation, gives us an overview of the heart of the good news. We are saved by the sheer goodness of God as a pure gift.

### LETTER TO THE ROMANS

In this letter we read, "Do you not know that God's kindness is an invitation to repent?" (Rom 2:4). It is because of God's mercy that He invites us to repent of our sins, not because of His wrath or judgment:

> The love of God has been poured into our hearts through the Holy Spirit who has been given to us. At the appointed time, when we were powerless, Christ died for us godless men. It is rare that anyone should lay down his life for a just man, though it is barely possible that for a good man someone may have the courage to die. It is precisely in this that God proves his love for us. [Rom 5:5-8.]

God shows the fullness of His merciful love in laying down His life for us (cf. John 3:16). It is all gift! (cf. Rom 3:24, 4:16).

In Romans, Saint Paul describes God's plan of mercy in choosing Israel, then cutting them off so that the Gentiles might also receive mercy (9–12). Saint Paul expresses the pain in his heart for his brothers, the Israelites, echoing the definition of *misericordia* given by Saint Thomas Aquinas.

God chose the Israelites as His people out of His mercy. "'I will show mercy to whomever I choose'. . . . So it is not a question of man's willing or doing but of God's mercy" (Rom 9:15-16).

God makes known His power to the Israelites "in order to make known the riches of his glory toward the vessels of his mercy" (cf. Rom 9:19-24).

Saint Paul then writes of God's universal mercy. "Here there is no difference between Jew and Greek; all have the same Lord, rich in mercy toward all who call upon him. For 'everyone who calls on the name of the Lord will be saved'" (Rom 10:12-13).

Saint Paul then asks if God has rejected His people: "Not at all! Rather, by their transgression, salvation has come to the Gentiles to stir Israel to envy. But if their transgression and their diminishing have meant riches for the Gentile world, how much more their full number" (Rom 11:11-12).

"Consider the kindness and the severity of God: severity toward those who fell, but God's kindness toward you, provided you remain in his kindness; if you do not, you too will be cut off. . . . blindness has come upon part of

Israel until the full number of Gentiles enter in, and then all of Israel will be saved. . ." (Rom 11:22, 25–26).

Now Saint Paul comes to the key point of his argumentation. God's plan is to have mercy on all: "Just as you were once disobedient to God and now have received mercy through their disobedience, so they have become disobedient, since God wished to show you mercy, that they too may receive mercy. God has imprisoned all in disobedience that he might have mercy on all" (Rom 11:30-32).

This is the statement of God's great plan and desire: MERCY ON ALL!

Saint Paul is so caught up in his development of the mystery of God's mercy that he bursts out into a great canticle of praise: "How deep are the riches and the wisdom and the knowledge of God! How inscrutable his judgments. How unsearchable his ways! For who has known the mind of the Lord? Or who has been his counselor? Who has given him anything so as to deserve return? For from him and through him and for him all things are. To him be glory forever. Amen" (Rom 11:33-36).

Saint Paul addresses the heart of his teaching on the mystery of God's mercy and exhorts us to show the fullness of mercy by the gift of our whole being, as a sacrifice to the Father: "And now, brothers, I beg you through the mercy of God to offer your bodies as a living sacrifice, holy and acceptable to God, your spiritual worship" (Rom 12:1).

Saint Paul challenges us to martyrdom in our daily lives. He continues to teach us how to use the various gifts of God that flow from His mercy, for the good of our neighbor and Church (cf. Rom 12:2-21). "Both in life and death we are the Lord's" (Rom 14:8). Chapters 12-15 of the Letter to the Romans teach us how to love and glorify God by our works and life of mercy. "The Gentiles glorify God because of his mercy" (Rom 15:9).

## SECOND LETTER OF SAINT PAUL TO THE CHURCH AT CORINTH

Saint Paul weaves the theme of mercy and love into his letters. In the second letter to the Church at Corinth he greets the Church with praise of the God of mercy. "Praised be God the Father of mercies, and the God of all consolations!" (2 Cor 1:3).

Saint Paul describes how we can comfort one another with the same merciful consolation we have received from the Lord (cf. 2 Cor 1:4-7). He speaks of the trials of his ministry and his attitude, "Because we possess this ministry through God's mercy, we do not give in to discouragement" (2 Cor 4:1).

He shows how, as ministers of reconciliation, we are ambassadors for Christ, or we might say, "ministers of his mercy" (2 Cor 5:16-21).

Saint Paul tells us of his twofold boast, his own weakness and God's power at work in him (cf. 2 Cor 12:7-10). This twofold boast can be echoed in our lives by the confession of our misery and sinfulness, on the one hand, and God's mercy, which is greater than all misery and sin, on the other.

## LETTER TO THE CHURCH AT EPHESUS

Saint Paul describes the great gift of mercy which we receive in our salvation:

But God who is rich in mercy, out of the great love with which he loved us, even when we were dead through our trespasses, made us alive together with Christ (by grace you have been saved) and raised us up with him, and made us sit with him in the heavenly places in Christ Jesus, that in the coming ages he might show the immeasurable riches of his grace in kindness toward us in Christ Jesus. [Eph 2:4-7.]

It is from this text that Pope John Paul II took the name of his encyclical *Dives in Misericordia*.

### LETTER TO THE CHURCH AT COLOSSAE

Saint Paul puts in a crisp phrase the meaning of our redemption by God's mercy, poured out on the Cross. "Through him [the beloved Son] we have redemption, the forgiveness of our sins" (Col 1:14). "It pleased God to make absolute fullness reside in him and by means of him, to reconcile everything in his person, both on earth and in the heavens, making peace through the blood of his cross" (Col 1:19-20).

Saint Paul exhorts us to live a life of mercy: "Because you are God's chosen ones, holy and beloved, clothe yourselves with heartfelt mercy, kindness, humility, meekness, and patience. Bear with one another; forgive grievances you have against one another, forgive as the Lord has forgiven you" (Col 3:12–13).

### LETTERS TO THE CHURCH AT THESSALONICA

Saint Paul pleads for growth in holiness and then prays for love, the Lord's mercy poured out:

And may the Lord increase you and make you overflow with love for one another and for all, even as our love does for you. May he strengthen your hearts, making them blameless and holy before our God and Father at the coming of our Lord Jesus with all his holy ones. [1 Thess 3:12-13.]

He encourages the church, "May our Lord Jesus Christ himself, and may God our Father who loved us and in his mercy gave us eternal consolation and hope, console your hearts and strengthen them for every good work and word" (2 Thess 2:16-17).

In praying this blessing Paul teaches us the works of mercy, in deed, word, and prayer. How beautifully this teaching is echoed in the diary of Blessed Faustina (cf. *Diary*, 742).

## LETTERS TO TIMOTHY

Saint Paul thanks Christ Jesus for having treated him mercifully in his conversion and he declares,

You can depend on this as worthy of full acceptance: that Jesus Christ came into the world to save sinners. Of these I myself am the worst. But on that very account I was dealt with mercifully, so that in me, as an extreme case, Jesus Christ might display all his patience, and I might become an example to those who later would have faith in him and gain everlasting life. [1 Tim 1:15–16.]

## LETTER TO TITUS

Again Saint Paul refers to the mercy of God in his conversion, and so ours:

When the kindness and love of God our Savior appeared, he saved us; not because of any righteous deeds we have done, but *because of his mercy*. He saved us through the baptism of new birth and renewal of the Holy Spirit. This Spirit he lavished on us through Jesus Christ our Savior, that we might be justified by his grace and become heirs, in hope, of eternal life. You can depend on this to be true. [Titus 3:4-8.]

"You can depend on this"! We have been made heirs of eternal life by the gift of His mercy!

Saint Paul teaches that by our faith in Jesus Christ, by our trust in Him we receive mercy which saves us, forgives us, and makes us heirs in hope, in Christ Jesus, of eternal life. Then, fortified with this mercy which we received as a gift from God, we are to be merciful to one another in deeds, words, and prayers. This theme is developed by Saint James.

LETTER OF SAINT JAMES

Saint James, in his blunt, straightforward way, writes of judgment, mercy, and good works:

Always speak and act as men destined for judgment under the law of freedom. Merciless is the judgment on the man who has not shown mercy; but mercy triumphs over judgment. My brothers, what good is it to profess faith without practicing it? Such faith has no power to save one, has it? . . . Be assured then, that faith without works is as dead as a body without breath. [James 2:12–14, 17.]

Since we have received mercy by our faith, we are to put it into practice and be merciful, even as our heavenly Father (cf. Luke 6:36).

Saint Peter describes our new birth of hope of salvation in Christ Jesus, received in baptism, as a gift of mercy: "Praised be the God and Father of our Lord Jesus Christ, he who in his great mercy gave us a new birth. . ." (1 Pet 1:3).

Further he describes the Church as a "chosen race, a royal priesthood, a holy nation, a people he claims for his own" (1 Pet 2:9), and he shows that this is the effect of God's mercy. "Once you were no people, but now you are God's people; once there was no mercy for you, but now you have found mercy" (1 Pet 2:10).

## LETTERS OF SAINT JOHN

Saint John writes of God's love for us and the love we are to have for one another that shows we love God. When Saint John speaks of love, we can easily substitute the word "mercy," that is, God's love poured out for us. Pope John Paul II in his encyclical seems to support the use of mercy for love when he calls mercy "love's second name" (*Dives in Misericordia*, n. 7).

With apologies to Saint John we could read his first letter using "mercy" in place of the word "love" (adapted from 1 John 4:7-11):

> Beloved, merciful ones, let us be merciful to one another because mercy is of God; everyone who is merciful is begotten of God. The man without mercy has known nothing of God, for God is mercy. God's mercy was revealed in our midst in this way: He sent his only Son to the world that we might have life through him. Mercy, then, consists in this: Not that we have had mercy on

48

God, but that he has had mercy on us and sent his Son as an offering for our sins. Merciful ones, if God has shown us mercy, so we must show the same mercy to one another.

From this we see that the command of Jesus to love one another as Christ has loved us (cf. John 13:34) is the parallel command recorded by Saint Luke, "Be merciful, even as your heavenly Father is merciful" (Luke 6:36). It is the other side of the coin: one side is mercy, the other is love. Both commands give us the same standard or measure of love, the Lord Jesus.

Letter of Saint Jude

Saint Jude exhorts the Church to receive God's mercy and to use it:

> Beloved, grow strong in your holy faith through prayer in the Holy Spirit. Persevere in God's love and welcome the mercy of Our Lord Jesus Christ which leads to eternal life. Correct those who are confused; the others you must rescue, snatching them from the fire. [Jude 20-23.]

Mercy is at the heart of the message of the Epistles. Receive the gift of God's mercy with trust and use that same mercy toward one another.

# 8

# Mercy: The Heart of the Letter to the Hebrews

IN MY STUDY OF MERCY in the Scriptures, I made a most exciting discovery when I realized the centrality of mercy and trust in the Letter to the Hebrews. Fr. Seraphim Michalenko, M.I.C., suggested I read the work of Fr. Albert Vanhoye, S.J., rector of the Biblical Institute in Rome. Father Vanhoye shows that the Letter to the Hebrews is a masterpiece of the New Testament developing the role and our need for the Eternal High Priest, Jesus Christ. My reflections are drawn from two of his works, *Structure and Message of the Epistle to the Hebrews* (Rome: Editrice Pontificio Istituto Biblico, 1989) and *Old Testament Priests and the New Priest: According to the New Testament* (Petersham, Massachusetts: St. Bede's Publications, 1980).

The overall movement of the Letter to the Hebrews is summed up in two sketches. The first: God in Christ Jesus descended to become man, revealing the fullness of His mercy. Man by trust in Christ Jesus ascends to God.

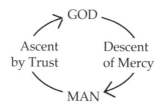

The second: Christ as High Priest bridges the abyss between the holiness of God and the misery of man. The distance between God's transcendent holiness and His extreme humility on the Cross is the measure of His mercy. The distance between our true state of misery, our humble state, and God's holiness is bridged by our trust in His mercy, trust in the Divine Mercy, Jesus Christ.

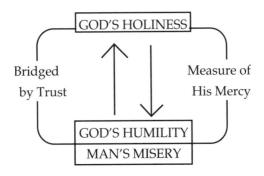

By His immolation on the Cross, as both priest and victim, Christ's humanity was transformed into a new humanity, a new tent, a new temple, a new covenant, giving us a new heart (cf. Heb 8:10; 10:15-18). Man needs a new heart which can only be given by the humanity of Jesus. The humanity of Jesus (His Body) is divinized at the moment of death as it passes through the veil.

Unbelief is *the* sin. *Trust* is the undoing of sin (cf. Heb 3:12-13).

According to Father Vanhoye, the Letter to the Hebrews is a highly structured development of overlapping themes which culminate in Christ's being made perfect by His sacrifice and thus becoming the source of mercy and salvation for us.

One way to outline the Letter to the Hebrews is simply to list the principle points:

· Christ is High Priest (cf. 2:17; 5:9–10; 7:1-28).
· He is worthy of *trust* (cf. 3:1–4:14).
· He is *merciful* (cf. 4:15-5:10).
· His humanity is transformed and perfected (cf. 5:9-10).
· He is made High Priest (cf. 7:1-28), glorified (cf. 8:1-9:28) and now is the new tent, the new sacrifice.
· He is transformed by His
    Obedience (cf. 4:15-5:10)
    Reverent plea (cf. 8:1-9:28)
    Passion-death-resurrection, mercy

· He becomes like His brethren and so is a true mediator (cf. 2:17).
· He offers Himself by the Eternal Spirit (cf. 9:14).
· He transforms us so that we have access to the Father (cf. 9:11-14). We have a new relationship to the Father (cf. 9:24-28). We are sanctified by His blood and are given salvation (cf. 10:1-18).
· Therefore, we are called to:
    faith and endurance (cf. 11:1-12:13)
    to walk the straight paths (cf. 12:14-13:18)

What amazed me was the discovery that the message of the Letter to the Hebrews is the message our Lord gave to Blessed Faustina which she recorded in her diary! God is merciful and He is worthy of all our trust!

Blessed Faustina's spiritual life reflects the same message of the letter: humble obedience to the will of God; offering herself with Christ as a victim-host for the salvation of souls; glorifying His mercy by deeds, words, and prayer; and pleading with her prayers and sufferings for mercy on the whole world.

Tables of comparison between the Letter to the Hebrews and *Divine Mercy in My Soul: The Diary of the Servant of God Sister M. Faustina Kowalska* can be found in appendix A. My study of the two texts strongly confirms the point of this book: mercy is the heart of the Gospel as well as the heart of the Letter to the Hebrews.

# 9

## The Heart of Mercy

WHAT IS THE HEART OF MERCY? The heart of mercy is the Heart of Jesus, the Sacred, Merciful Heart of Jesus, the human-divine Heart pierced on the Cross, the Heart from which flowed blood and water as a fount of mercy for us (cf. John 19:34). The Heart of Jesus is the heart of the Gospel and the heart of mercy.

The Heart of Jesus pierced on the Cross is not only the summary of the Gospel but is also the source of all mercy. This sweeping statement is verified by the Sacred Scriptures, the Fathers of the Church, a long list of Popes, and the revelations of Blessed Faustina.

Professor Timothy T. O'Donnell, in his thorough study of the origins and the history of the devotion to the Sacred Heart of Jesus, *Heart of the Redeemer* (San Francisco: Ignatius Press, 1992), shows how the Fathers of the Church in the first six centuries based their devotion to the humanity of Jesus and His passion on a number of texts of Sacred Scripture which later developed into the devotion to the Sacred Heart of Jesus. These same texts are also the foundation for the devotion to the Divine Mercy:

1. Christ is the source of living waters (cf. John 7:36-39), the rock from whom the water of the Spirit flows, and the Lamb, the source of living water (cf. Exod 17:6; Rev 5:6).

2. Christ is the second spiritual Adam (cf. 1 Cor 15:45) from whose side the Church is born.

3. The blood and water from the side of Christ symbolize the two chief Sacraments of the Church: Baptism and Eucharist (cf. John 19:34).

4. Saint John's resting on the Heart of Jesus drew living waters (cf. John 13:23).

5. Jesus accepted suffering through His merciful love (cf. Psalm 56; John 3:16; 13:1; Heb 12:2).

6. We are to follow in the footsteps of Christ, e.g., Galations 2:20: "It is no longer I that live, but Christ lives in me."

7. Commentaries on the Song of Songs nurture the devotion, e.g., You have wounded my heart (cf. 4:9); Put me as a seal upon your heart (cf. 8:6).

These texts are the foundation of the devotion to the Heart of Jesus. But they are more. They are a summary of the Gospel According to John. Fr. Eduoard Glotin, S.J., in *Sign of Salvation: Sacred Heart of Jesus* (New Hyde Park, New York: Apostleship of Prayer, 1989) shows that the pierced Heart of Jesus is the final sign of the book of signs.

Saint John presents a series of signs, miraculous events in the life of Jesus, that have deep mystical meaning: e.g., the wedding at Cana, the woman at the well, multiplication of the loaves and fish, the curing of the blind man, and the raising of Lazarus from the dead. The piercing of the side of Jesus is the greatest sign on which the whole Gospel is structured. After death comes life under the signs of blood and water. At the hour of the sacrifice of the paschal lamb whose bones were not broken, the true Lamb of God is lifted up. All who would gaze upon Him whom they pierced (cf. John 19:37) could be drawn to Himself (cf. John 12:32). All this was done so that we would believe and cry out with Saint Thomas, "My Lord and my God!" (John 20:28).

The Gospel According to John is structured to point to this final and greatest sign. Saint John the Baptist points to Jesus as the Lamb of God who takes away the sins of the world (cf. John 1:29), as the one to baptize in the Holy Spirit (cf. John 1:33), and as God's chosen one (cf. John 1:34). The prophetic pointing of Saint John the Baptist is fulfilled in the handing over of the spirit of mercy, the Lamb of God, the piercing of the Heart of Jesus, from which the blood and water gushed forth to wash away our sins. We, too, with Saint Thomas, can put our hands into the pierced side of the risen Jesus and cry out in trusting faith, "My Lord and my God!" (John 20:28).

Yes, Jesus is the rock that was struck (cf. Exod 17:6) from which living water gushed forth (cf. John 7:37-39) as a fountain of mercy for us and for the whole world.

The Heart of Jesus developed as a key focus of devotion through the teachings of saints and mystics, coming to a high point in the revelations of Our Lord to Saint Margaret Mary Alacoque in 1673. The message and devotion to the Sacred Heart of Jesus received the public approval of the Church from Pope Leo XIII and every pope in the twentieth century.

In 1899, Pope Leo XIII consecrated the world to the Sacred Heart of Jesus and approved the Litany of the Sacred Heart. Each invocation is taken from Sacred Scripture.

In 1928, Pope Pius XI in his encyclical *Miserentissimus Redemptor* (*Most Compassionate Redeemer*) described the devotion as "the very summary of our religion" (n. 4).

In 1956, Pope Pius XII issued *Haurietis Aquas*, the encyclical on the Sacred Heart, in which he stressed that the infinite love of God for the human race is the principal object of the devotion (I.C.). It is "a devotion to the mystery of God's merciful love for the human race. In this special manifestation Christ pointed to His Heart, with definite and repeated words, as the symbol by which men should be attracted to a knowledge and recognition of His love; and, at the same time He established it as a sign or pledge of mercy and grace for the needs of the Church of our times" (n. 97).

Pope John XXIII wrote of his personal devotion to the Sacred Heart: "The devotion to the Heart of Jesus has grown with me all my life . . . I am determined to give myself no peace until I can truly say I am absorbed into the Heart of Jesus" (*Journal of a Soul* [Garden City, New York: Image Books], pp. 157-158).

Pope Paul VI, elected on the Feast of the Sacred Heart in 1963, affirms and explains the teaching of the Second Vatican Council on devotions: "Popular devotions of the Christian people, provided they conform to the laws and norms of the Church, are to be highly recommended, especially where they are ordered by the Apostolic See" (*Sacrosanctum Concilium*, n. 13).

Pope Paul VI in *Investigabiles Divitates Christi* and *Diserti Interoretes* explicitly shows that the devotion to the Sacred Heart is the fulfillment of the teachings of the Second Vatican Council. He uses very strong language to show its importance in our times:

Thus it is absolutely necessary that the faithful venerate and honor this Heart, in the expression of their private piety as well as in the services of public cult, for of His fullness we have all received; and they must learn perfectly from Him how they are to live in order to answer the demand of our time. [*Diserti Interoretes.*]

Pope John Paul II has a personal and profound devotion to the Sacred Heart and to the Divine Mercy. This is shown most clearly in his encyclical *Dives in Misericordia.* He states that the Heart of Jesus pierced for us on the Cross is the revelation of the mercy of the Father, and this revelation is the central message of the Messiah:

The Church seems to profess and venerate the mercy of God in an extraordinary way when she turns to the Heart of Jesus. In fact, it is precisely this drawing close to Christ in the mystery of His Heart which allows us to stop and dwell on this central point [a point in a sense central and also most accessible on the human level] . . . the revelation of the Father's merciful love, a revelation which makes up the central content of the messianic mission of the Son of man. [N. 13.]

This is one of the sweeping summaries of his encyclical and a summary of the Gospel and mission of Jesus. The pierced, Merciful Heart of Jesus is the revelation of God's plan of salvation to "have mercy on all" (Rom 11:32). Statements like the one quoted above have led me to define God's mercy, His love, as His Holy Spirit of love poured out through the pierced Heart of Jesus for us miserable sinners. His mercy gushes out as a flood of blood and water on us and on the whole world. His mercy *is* life-giving love poured out through the pierced Heart of Jesus.

The Merciful Heart of Jesus is also a summary of the devotion and message of the Divine Mercy. I came to see this in the life of Blessed Faustina. She recorded her personal devotion to the Merciful Heart of Jesus in her diary. Blessed Faustina's special devotion to the Merciful Heart of Jesus unified her devotion to the Divine Mercy. It was based on the union of her heart with the Heart of Jesus. She was challenged by the Lord to model her life on the Heart of Jesus from the crib to the Cross.

Her devotion expressed itself in gazing upon the Heart of Jesus, especially in the Eucharist, taking refuge in His Heart, resting upon it, and glorifying His mercy by her prayers, sufferings, writings, and her works of mercy.

Each of the five special vessels of mercy—the Feast of Divine Mercy, the image of the Merciful Savior, the Chaplet of Divine Mercy, the Novena, and the Hour of Great Mercy (three o'clock) which our Lord designed and asked Blessed Faustina to make known, is an expression of His Merciful Heart and summed up in the Heart of Jesus.

Yes, mercy is the heart of the Gospel and the heart of mercy is the Merciful, Sacred Heart of Jesus pierced for us.

"O Blood and Water, which gushed forth from the Heart of Jesus as a fount of Mercy for us, I trust in You" (*Diary*, 187).

# 10

# Trust and Mercy:  The Heart of the Good News

IN THIS CHAPTER I bring together the essential features of the Good News in order to see them in the light of God's mercy. This chapter is a bird's-eye view of the key role of trust and Divine Mercy.  Some repetition is necessary to show the relationship of the parts to the whole and to give each part a new emphasis.  Each feature will be presented in summary form so that the overall picture will become clear. As with putting together the pieces of a jigsaw puzzle, the final picture is the goal.

*The Good News: The* Good News is that Divine Mercy is present and comes in the person of Jesus Christ, our Lord. Our response is to trust Him.

*Mercy:* Divine Mercy is forgiving love. It is life-giving love that has been poured out from the pierced Heart of Jesus.

*Trust:* Trust is a living faith, a total reliance upon saving truth—Jesus Christ who is Mercy itself.

*Salvation:* Salvation is God's merciful love given to sinners.  Jesus came to save sinners. "I have not come to call the righteous but sinners to repentance" (Luke 5:32).

*Redemption:* Saint Paul writes: "Through him [Christ] we have redemption, the forgiveness of sin" (Col 1:14).

Forgiveness of sin is what God's mercy and redemption are all about.

*Sinners:* Sinners, the miserable, and the humble are the prime recipients of God's mercy. "Abiding compunction for sin" is the necessary condition for receiving God's love.

*Proclamation:* Jesus proclaimed the good news of God saying: "The time is fulfilled and the kingdom of God is at hand; repent and believe in the gospel" (Mark 1:15).

*The Time Is Fulfilled:* Now is the time to turn to God's mercy with trust, while there is time for mercy. This is the trust of the message of Divine Mercy as revealed to Blessed Faustina (e.g., *Diary*, 83, 848, 1160).

*Repent:* To repent means to turn from self-centeredness and from sin and turn with trust to the living God, to the God who is Mercy itself. The purpose of our repenting is to receive mercy.

*Kingdom:* The Kingdom of God is at hand, wherever the Holy Spirit is present. It is the presence of His Merciful Love (cf. Pope John Paul II, *Redemptor Hominis*). Jesus came to make the Kingdom of God present by making mercy present. That mercy is made present in our hearts by the Holy Spirit (cf. Rom 5:5). The Kingdom of God *is* within our hearts.

*Believe:* To believe is to have *living faith;* it is to trust. It is the mercy of God made present, the Good News. So we respond with the cry, "Jesus, I trust in You!"

*Commandment of Love:* To love God is to trust Him, to allow Him to love us (cf. 1 John 4:10). To love our neighbor is to be merciful to him as God is merciful to us.

The new commandment Jesus gave us at the Last Supper: "A new commandment I give to you, that you love one another; even as I have loved you, that you love one another" (John 13:34), has another expression in the Gospel According to Luke: "Be merciful, even as your Father is merciful" (Luke 6:36). Both of these commands, to love and to be merciful, are based on God's own love and mercy for us.

*Parables and Events of Trust and Mercy:* Jesus described the mercy of the Father in the parables of the good Samaritan (cf. Luke 10:30-37), the prodigal son (cf. Luke 15:11-32), the lost sheep (cf. Luke 15:1-7), and the merciless official (cf. Matt 18:21-35).

The events of forgiveness of sin such as the paralytic man (cf. Matt 9:1-8), and the widow giving her gift of a mite, giving her all (cf. Luke 21:1-4), teach us about God's mercy and our need to trust.

*The Events of Holy Thursday:* The night before He died Jesus revealed His merciful love to His disciples and established the Eucharist as the seal of His love. This Last Supper in the upper room was a canticle of love (cf. John 13-17). He left Himself in the miracle of mercy, the Eucharist.

*Good Friday:* Jesus shared His love to the utmost on the Cross (cf. John 13:1). After His death His side was pierced and blood and water gushed forth as a fount of mercy for us (cf. John 19:34).

*Blood and Water:* There is no forgiveness of sin, no mercy, without the shedding of blood (cf. Heb 9:22). The blood of Christ that is shed for the forgiveness of our sins (the words of consecration of the wine at Mass) is no longer the blood and water of the animals that Moses sprinkled as a sealing of the covenant (cf. Heb 9:19), but the blood and water from the side of Christ, the blood of the new and eternal covenant.

*Easter Sunday and Resurrection:* On Easter Sunday night the risen and victorious Jesus appeared to His disciples (cf. John 20). He greeted them with *shalom,* peace, the peace that comes from the fullness of all blessings, the fullness of mercy. He showed His wounds, the signs of victory, and even as He was sent by His Father, He commissioned His disciples to reveal mercy. To make possible this mandate of mercy He breathed on them the Holy Spirit so that they might forgive sins. This was a revelation and an empowering of mercy, mercy, mercy!

The blessing of mercy is given and received, and the commission of mercy is to be given to others, especially in the forgiveness of sins.

*Ascension:* The Ascension is a blessing, a promise, and a departure. It is a blessing of peace and mercy accompanied by a promise to send the Holy Spirit and a promise to return again, in order to bring His mercy to those who eagerly await Him (cf. Heb 9:28).

*Pentecost and the Upper Room:* The Holy Spirit as a spirit of fire and love is poured into our hearts (cf. Acts 2; Rom 5:5). Mercy itself is poured into our hearts by the gifts of the Holy Spirit.

*Holy Spirit:* One of the great works of the Holy Spirit is to convict us of sin, to convict us of the world within us. The Holy Spirit convicts us not in order to condemn us but in order to bring us to the source of all mercy, the pierced Heart of Jesus on the Cross (cf. John 16:7-11 and John Paul II's *Dominum et Vivificantem* (*Lord and Giver of Life*), his encyclical on the Holy Spirit).

By the work of the Holy Spirit our sin and misery meet the mercy of God.

*Covenant:* God's solemn promise to Israel that He would be their God and that they would be His people is a covenant of mercy. The promise is a family bond of kinship.

The new covenant, established by the shedding of the blood of Jesus, adds to the covenant of mercy the readiness to forgive. Like the father in the parable of the prodigal son, the Heavenly Father searches us out to find, to forgive, to reestablish our family bonds, to restore our dignity as sons and daughters of the Father—all because of His merciful, forgiving love.

*Church:* The assembly of the "being saved sinners" is the sign of the Kingdom of God's presence among us. By trusting in the mercy of God, the Church makes present that mercy as a witness to the world. By being merciful (cf. Luke 6:36) the Good News becomes believable to the world and present in our time.

The Church is a human, divine organism, the living mystical Body of Christ, and not just a human organization. It shows the transforming power of mercy. Our sin and misery are the very human stuff that is transformed into saving mercy for ourselves and others.

*Baptism:* The Sacraments are the transforming agents established by Christ to give grace and mercy. In our Creed we profess our faith in one baptism for the forgiveness of sins. By our baptism we are bonded into the family covenant of God, the Church.

*Confirmation:* In Confirmation we are strengthened by the gift of the Holy Spirit in order to be witnesses to Jesus Christ. Confirmation is a gift of mercy to enable us to become mature Christians, merciful even as our Father is merciful.

*Holy Eucharist:* The Holy Eucharist is the miracle of mercy present, offered in sacrifice, and given in a communion of loving mercy.

*Reconciliation:* Confession or Penance is the work of the Holy Spirit which bring us mercy, the forgiveness of our sins. The very words the Church places on the lips of the priest speak of this mercy:

> God, the Father of mercies, through the death and resurrection of His Son has reconciled the world to himself and sent the Holy Spirit among us for the forgiveness of sins; through the ministry of the Church may God give you pardon and peace, and I absolve you from your sins in the name of the Father, and of the Son, and of the Holy Spirit.

Truly this Sacrament is a tribunal of mercy and not a tribunal of judgment and condemnation.

*Response to the Gift of Mercy:* How shall we respond to the gift of God's mercy? We can respond by living out Saint Paul's exhortation: "Rejoice always. Pray without ceasing. In all circumstances give thanks, for this is the will of God in Christ Jesus regarding you all" (1 Thess 5:16-18).

Truly, God's mercy is a gift to us. We are challenged to receive it with trust and then give it away, especially to those in need. Yes, trust and mercy are at the heart of the Good News.

PART THREE

BAPTIZED IN HIS MERCY

# 11

## Baptize Us with Your Mercy

AT MASS on the Feast of the Baptism of Our Lord, January 12, 1992, as I was announcing the closing hymn *Mercy, Lord* (an English version of the ancient Latin hymn *Parce Domine*), I prayed, "Lord, baptize us in Your mercy!" After Mass, I knelt for a time of thanksgiving and I was puzzled by what I had just prayed, "Baptize us in Your mercy." The phrase kept resounding in my head and heart and I wondered if it was a new insight or just a happy twist of words.

When something like this happens, I take out my journal and jot down related thoughts. The more I wrote, the more insights surfaced in my mind. I shared them with a student for the priesthood who was living and praying with me at Divine Mercy House in Steubenville. We wondered at the richness of the phrase and asked ourselves, what would be the experience of being baptized in His mercy? In the days that followed, new insights, new dimensions and expansions of my initial notes developed. I shared the phrase with many others.

One day after a holy hour those present shared about their understanding and experience of Divine Mercy. With each sharing a new excitement about the meaning of being baptized in His mercy grew in my heart and in my mind.

One woman shared an insight into Mary's role: Mary received mercy for us at the Cross. In response to this reflection on being baptized in His mercy, I reread the section on Mary, the "Mother of Mercy" in *Dives in Misericordia* (n. 9).

At first, I was hesitant to write about the new concept of being baptized in His mercy. But during Mass one morning, during the consecration of the wine, as I prayed the words of institution, I heard in my heart, "Write on the baptism in mercy." The word was a peaceful and gentle word, but a word that urged me to begin.

Obedient to the word, I outlined the various topics that explain baptism in His mercy. The meaning, value, and experience, along with the resulting mission and the prayers that flow from it developed. My outline included four encyclicals of Pope John Paul II, the scriptural ways of speaking of the fullness of Baptism, and Mary's role as Mother of Mercy both at the Incarnation and at the Cross.

I prayed frequently, "Lord, baptize me in Your mercy! I need to know and experience what this means so that I can share it with others, for the salvation of souls and for Your glory."

# 12

## "I Have a Baptism to Receive" (Luke 12:50)

JESUS experienced a baptism that was threefold: a baptism in water, a baptism in the Spirit, and a baptism in blood. Saint John in his first letter says these three are one (cf. 1 John 5:8).

The more I have reflected on the meaning of this three-fold baptism of Jesus, the more I see it as a total immersion in mercy, "a baptism in mercy." The word baptism in the Greek language means to immerse or to dip, or even to plunge. It is the purpose of these reflections to plunge into the possible meaning and significance of the rich phrase "baptism in His mercy."

Jesus was baptized in water in the river Jordan by Saint John the Baptist. Jesus was not a sinner in need of repentance but, in humble obedience to the will of the Father, He shared His solidarity with all of us who are sinners. The Gospels According to Matthew (cf. 3:13-17), Mark (cf. 1:9-11), and Luke (cf. 3:21-22) record Jesus as being baptized by Saint John the Baptist, while the Gospel According to John does so by implication (cf. John 1:28-34).

Jesus was baptized in the Holy Spirit after coming out of the water. The Spirit of God descended like a dove and hovered over Him and a voice from heaven said, "This is my beloved Son. My favor rests on him" (Matt 3:16-17).

Jesus is described as the one who will baptize us in the Holy Spirit (cf. John 1:33) and in fire (cf. Matt 3:11; Luke 3:16).

Jesus was baptized in blood. He foretold his baptism in pain and in blood when He responded to the request of James and John to sit at His right hand in heaven, "Can you drink the cup I shall drink or be baptized in the same bath of pain as I?" (Mark 10:38). In the Gospel According to Luke, Jesus expresses His desire for this baptism to be accomplished: "I have come to light a fire on the earth. How I wish the blaze were ignited! I have a baptism to receive. What anguish I feel until it is over!" (Luke 12:49-50).

Jesus came in humble obedience to the will of the Father, giving Himself in a total immersion, a full plunge into that will: "I have come to do your will. . ." (Heb 10:7). And a body was provided for Him so that He would fully plunge into the will of the Father in offering Himself for all (cf. 1 John 4:10).

This total offering is the love with which the Father loves us. "God so loved us that he gave his only Son" (John 3:16), and this love consists in this: "Not that we have loved God, but that he has loved us and has sent his Son as an offering for our sins" (1 John 4:10).

And this love is His mercy, mercy totally poured out as offering for our sins.

Jesus came to reveal the mercy of the Father and to make it present. The fullness of the revelation of God's mercy took place on the Cross (cf. *Dives in Misericordia*, nn. 7, 8). Jesus revealed the fullness of the Father's mercy by being baptized in that mercy, plunged into the water, the

Spirit, and the blood. The love of the Father that creates us is mercy; the love of the Son that redeems us is mercy; the love of the Holy Spirit that sanctifies us is mercy. There is one love and one mercy.

Saint Matthew beautifully closes his Gospel with the mission mandate of Jesus to His disciples to baptize in the name of the triune loving God:

> Full authority has been given to me both in heaven and earth; go, therefore, and make disciples of all the nations. Baptize them in the name of the Father, and of the Son, and of the Holy Spirit. Teach them to carry out everything I have commanded you. And know I am with you always, until the end of the world! [Matt 28:18-20.]

The experience of baptism for Saint Paul is a sharing in the death and resurrection of Jesus (cf. Col 2:12). By baptism we share in the full revelation of the Father's mercy in Christ, who Himself was fully baptized in that mercy and so became the source of mercy to all who call upon Him (cf. Rom 10:12).

By our full baptism we share in the threefold baptism of Christ. It is important to recall that baptism in Sacred Scripture refers to the full initiation into Christ which includes the three Sacraments of Baptism, Confirmation, and Holy Eucharist. When we are baptized into Christ, we are baptized into the water, the Spirit, and the blood, and these three are one.

The single word that describes the oneness of the threefold baptism is "mercy." This mercy is God's love poured out on us sinners, poured out through the Merciful Heart of Jesus pierced for us on the Cross. After He handed over His spirit (John 19:30), His side was pierced and out flowed blood and water (cf. John 19:34). Out flowed His mercy.

73

To my delight, I found that Saint Catherine of Siena, a doctor of the Church, asked our Lord: "Why, gentle, spotless Lamb, did You want Your Heart to be pierced and parted, since You were already dead when Your side was opened?" He answered: "I wanted you to see My inmost Heart, so that you would know that I love you more than finite suffering [of my human body] could show." He then developed His answer by describing the oneness of Christian baptism of water, the Spirit, and the blood, by which we are continually to receive mercy from His Heart (*The Dialogue of the Seraphic Virgin Catherine of Siena*, trans. Algar Thorold [Westminster, Maryland: Newman Press], n. 75).

When we are baptized into Christ, into His death and resurrection (cf. Rom 6:3-4), we are baptized in His mercy! Our baptism in His mercy is a total plunge into the water, the Spirit, and the blood. When we are baptized in His mercy, we receive the fullness of the baptism Jesus so desired (cf. Luke 12:50).

Baptism in His mercy is a total plunge into the Spirit and fire, a total plunge into the bath of pain and blood of Christ on the Cross. To be baptized in His mercy is to be ignited with the zeal and desire of Christ for the baptism He was to receive (ibid.).

To be baptized in His mercy is to be identified with Christ in being perfected by His obedient suffering (cf. Heb 5:8-9). We can move beyond the foundations of our faith to the maturity of being priest-victims with Him (cf. Col 1:24; Heb 6:1-3) for the salvation of souls.

To be baptized in His mercy is to become channels of His mercy to others (cf. 2 Cor 5:17-21). To be baptized in His mercy means to be merciful even as our heavenly Father is merciful (cf. Luke 6:36).

# 13

## How Am I to Be Baptized in His Mercy?

HOW DO I become baptized in the Lord's mercy? How will I know that I am? What effect will it have on my life? These are important questions. Some of the answers have already been touched on in previous chapters but, because of the importance of the questions, it is valuable to consider them more fully.

How do I become baptized in the Lord's mercy? Mercy is a gracious gift of God. By His mercy He plunges us into the infinite ocean of His mercy as pure gift, pouring out His love for what we do not deserve. Since it is a gift, we can ask for it with trust. Trust is the vessel with which we receive His mercy; trust is the condition that gives God the permission to be merciful to us. He waits upon our freely asking for mercy so that He can act freely and not violate our freedom that He created. So we ask in prayer: Lord, fill me with Your mercy that I may be merciful. Lord, baptize me in Your mercy that I may radiate Your mercy.

The Lord hears and honors our prayers as we continue to ask, to seek, and to knock according to His instructions (cf. Luke 11:9). I continue to pray for baptism in His mercy so that I may know and experience His mercy more and more.

How will we know that we are baptized in His mercy? This question led me to the Sacred Scriptures for clues.

Interestingly enough, what I found was a description of how to respond to suffering:

> For the sake of the joy that lay before him, Jesus endured the cross, heedless of its shame. [Heb 12:2.]

> Even now I find my joy in the sufferings I endure for you. In my own flesh I fill up what is lacking in the sufferings of Christ for the sake of his body, the Church. [Col 1:24.]

> Rejoice in the measure that you share in Christ's sufferings. [1 Pet 4:13.]

> It is your special privilege to take Christ's part—not only to believe in him but also to suffer for him. [Phil 1:29.]

The common element in these passages is joy: joy in suffering for the sake of Christ, for the sake of others. There can be joy, not in the pain, but in the meaning and the value for others. Our suffering can mean mercy and salvation for others!

Besides joy, the presence of peace and love characterize being baptized in the Lord's mercy. The peace is the peace that Christ gave to His Apostles on Easter Sunday night when He breathed the Holy Spirit upon them (cf. John 20:22). This is the love with which the Father loves us and which He has shown us in giving us His only Son. It is the love poured into our hearts through the gift of the Holy Spirit (cf. Rom 5:5).

If we have this peace, joy, and love in the midst of our sufferings, then we are experiencing His mercy and we know that we are baptized in it. Peace, joy, and love are the signs of the presence of God's mercy.

When we are fully baptized into Christ (cf. Gal 3:27) we will experience His mercy present in our hearts and flowing out to others. It is all gift and it is available for the asking.

What will be the effect of being baptized in His mercy? Saint Paul gives us the answer: "I have been crucified with Christ, and the life I live now is not my own. Christ is living in me. I still live my human life, but it is a life of faith in the Son of God, who loved me and gave himself for me" (Gal 2:19-20).

The effect of being baptized in His mercy is that we are transformed by His mercy to be His Body, to be "living Eucharist," transformed in order to be given for others. This baptism will mean that we will radiate His mercy to others because we are filled with His mercy, and we will then be able to be merciful even as our heavenly Father is merciful (cf. Luke 6:36). We will be merciful with His mercy and not just our own.

Yes, it will mean that our hearts will be pierced, not unlike Jesus and Mary on Calvary: Jesus' Heart was pierced by the lance; Mary, standing at the foot of the Cross, experienced her heart being pierced by compassion over the passion of her Son (cf. John 19:34; Luke 2:35).

The effect of being baptized in mercy will mean that we will be channels of God's mercy, ministers and ambassadors of merciful reconciliation (cf. 2 Cor 5:17-21).

Yes, baptism in mercy will mean accepting the cup the Lord offers us just as Jesus drank the cup the Father offered Him (cf. Mark 10:39; 14:36). It will mean saying a total and continuous "yes" with Jesus and with Mary, all for mercy and the salvation of souls.

Baptism in mercy will mean that we become living witnesses to the water, the Spirit, and the blood (cf. 1 John 5:8); witnesses to His mercy poured out. We will be transformed by the radiance of His water, blood, and Spirit that flowed out from His pierced side (cf. John 19:34).

Baptism in mercy will mean living the prayer our Lord taught to Blessed Faustina Kowalska as a means of offering her sufferings each day: "O Blood and Water which gushed forth from the Heart of Jesus as a Fount of mercy for us, I trust in You!" (*Diary*, 309).

Baptism in mercy will mean interceding for God's mercy for each event of the day, using "all prayers and petitions" (1 Tim 2:1), beginning with the greatest plea for mercy, holy Mass, and continuing with the Chaplet of Divine Mercy as a plea for mercy on the whole Church and world:

> Eternal Father, I offer You the Body and Blood, Soul and Divinity of Your dearly beloved Son, our Lord Jesus Christ, in atonement for our sins and those of the whole world.

> For the sake of His sorrowful Passion, have mercy on us and on the whole world.

This great plea for God's mercy, composed and designed by our Lord and taught to Blessed Faustina, can be applied to each moment with the simple plea of the heart: "Jesus, mercy!"

"Jesus, mercy!" is both an act of praise of Jesus who is Mercy itself, and a petition for mercy when we pray it at each moment, at each event, and at each thought. In this way we will be praying without ceasing (cf. 1 Thess 5:17) for mercy on all!

As we are baptized in His mercy, God accomplishes His great plan and desire for us, that we be transformed to be instruments to bring His mercy to all.

# 14

## Baptism in Divine Mercy:
## The Answer to Suffering

"SUFFERING AND PAIN" is the human condition of all of us. On a number of occasions I have asked thousands of people at conferences to answer three questions. By their show of hands the answers have been very clear. "How many have experienced Jesus in their lives?" A sea of hands goes up. "How many have experienced the Holy Spirit in their lives?" Again a sea of hands goes up, some with both hands raised. "How many have suffering and pain in their lives? Slowly, a sea of hands goes up again. "But how can this be," I would ask them, "since you just indicated that you have experienced Jesus and the Holy Spirit?" So I will ask the third question again, but this time as a negative question: "How many have neither suffering nor pain in their lives? Would you please raise your hands." No hands go up! I ask the people to look around and confirm the fact that no one raised a hand. We all have suffering and pain!

The first time I asked these questions was at a day of intercessory prayer at Manhattan College in the Bronx, New York. A woman stood up after the question and cried out with great anguish, "Help me! I'm suffering!" I still can hear that cry. I still can see her standing up to express her pain.

Many have experienced the forgiveness of Jesus and the healing of the Holy Spirit and yet experience suffering and pain! This is all part of the Gospel. I realize now that our experience of suffering is our Lord's way of inviting us to move on to the fullness of His threefold baptism of water, the Spirit, and the blood. Our experience of suffering is an invitation to be baptized in His mercy, to share in His suffering, and to be ministers of mercy to the miserable. The very word "mercy" in Latin is *misericordia*, as we have noted earlier. According to Saint Thomas Aquinas it literally means to have a "miserable heart." It means to have a pain in our heart over the pain of another, and to take pains to relieve that pain in others.

Pope John Paul II in his apostolic exhortation *On the Christian Meaning of Human Suffering* (*Salvifici Doloris*) says that Christ taught us two things about suffering: one, to do good to those who are suffering, and two, to do good with the suffering. And it is precisely in this that we need to be baptized in God's mercy. Unless we are filled with His mercy and transformed by His mercy we cannot embrace suffering for others with peace, joy, and love.

In and through our suffering, Christ is inviting us to participation in His priestly ministry as priest-victim. By His mercy we are given a new birth (cf. 1 Pet 1:3) and made into a royal priesthood (cf. 1 Pet 2:9). By His mercy we not only receive a new birth by baptismal water and the Holy Spirit (cf. John 3:4-5) but we receive the grace to offer our sufferings for Christ (cf. Phil 1:29) and for the Church (cf. Col 1:24), offering our "bodies as a living sacrifice holy and acceptable to God" (Rom 12:1).

This is the central teaching of the Second Vatican Council (cf. Karol Wojtyla, now John Paul II, in *Sources of Renewal:*

*A Commentary on Vatican II* [San Francisco: Harper & Row, 1979]). By baptism we are all a "royal priesthood" and together with the ordained priest we are to offer the Immaculate Victim to the Father, along with all our works, our joys, and our sufferings, in order to "consecrate the world itself to God" (*Lumen Gentium*, n. 34).

In order to do this, we need to be filled with and transformed by God's mercy. We need to be baptized in His mercy. The power and effectiveness of this kind of offering of our sufferings is taught very clearly by our Lord to Blessed Faustina in His "Conference on Sacrifice and Prayer" (cf. *Diary*, 1767). It is reproduced here in its entirety because of the power He ascribes to prayer and suffering.

> My daughter, I want to instruct you on how you are to rescue souls through sacrifice and prayer. You will save more souls through prayer and suffering than will a missionary through his teachings and sermons alone. I want to see you as a sacrifice of living love, which only then carries weight before Me. You must be annihilated, destroyed, living as if you were dead in the most secret depths of your being. You must be destroyed in that secret depth where the human eye has never penetrated; then will I find in you a pleasing sacrifice, a holocaust full of sweetness and fragrance. And great will be your power for whomever you intercede. Outwardly, your sacrifice must look like this: silent, hidden, permeated with love, imbued with prayer. I demand, My daughter, that your sacrifice be pure and full of humility, that I may find pleasure in it. I will not spare My grace, that you may be able to fulfill what I demand of you.
>
> I will now instruct you on what your holocaust shall consist of, in everyday life, so as to preserve you from

illusions. You shall accept all sufferings with love. Do not be afflicted if your heart often experiences repugnance and dislike for sacrifice. All its power rests in the will, and so these contrary feelings, far from lowering the value of the sacrifice in My eyes, will enhance it. Know that your body and soul will often be in the midst of fire. Although you will not feel My presence on some occasions, I will always be with you. Do not fear; My grace will be with you. . . . [*Diary*, 1767.]

Earlier Blessed Faustina recorded the details around the "exclusive privilege" of drinking from the Lord's cup which He gave her. "The Lord said to me, 'I am taking you into My school for the whole of Lent. I want to teach you how to suffer.' I answered, 'With You, Lord, I am ready for everything.' And I heard a voice, 'You are allowed to drink from the cup from which I drink. I give you that exclusive privilege today. . .'" (*Diary*, 1626).

The mystery of suffering and evil is probably the greatest obstacle to not believing in God. Yet I have become convinced that the mystery of suffering holds within it the very answer to that mystery. Consider it in the following way. There are three things we can absolutely be sure of in this life: our death, our suffering, and God's mercy. That we all will die and we all will have suffering are obvious and proven facts. But God's mercy? The common objection is, "If God is so merciful, why am I suffering? It's impossible. It's a contradiction!" No, it is not impossible, nor is it a contradiction; rather it is a mysterious paradox. Yes, "God so loved the world [and all persons in it] that he gave his only begotten Son, that whoever believes in him may not die but may have eternal life" (John 3:16).

Out of His loving mercy Jesus embraced sin and suffering (cf. 1 Pet 2:21-24) in order to bring life to us who believe and who trust in His merciful love. Jesus transformed suffering to be the source of mercy. This is the mysterious paradox: Suffering is the source of saving love! (cf. John Paul II, *Dominum et Vivificantem*).

If we doubt that suffering is the source of mercy, we need only to gaze on Him whom they have pierced (cf. John 19:34ff.) and see the pierced Merciful Heart of Jesus as the source of all mercy. Blood and water flowed as a fount of mercy for us and the whole world. The very thing we seek to reject and run away from is the source of what we want and need: the peace, joy, and love of His mercy.

Man tries to escape from suffering and pain by every possible means—drugs, alcohol, raiding the ice-box, watching more television, going on another trip, and on and on. And yet within the mystery of suffering is the paradox of God's mercy, the answer to the great question that plagues mankind: "Why evil and suffering? Why me?"

To experience this answer of God's mercy we need to receive His mercy with trust. We need to be filled and transformed by His mercy. We need to be baptized in His mercy so that we can embrace our present sufferings with peace, joy, and love for the sake of others, so "God may have mercy on all" (Rom 11:32).

Our embracing of suffering and pain does not mean that we should neglect normal health and medical rules. Rather it means we make use of the sufferings as long as we have them. This embrace of sufferings is not a masochism which seeks pleasure in the pain; it is a seeking of that mercy which flows out to those in misery. And so we rejoice! Our embracing suffering is not a way of asking for more sufferings; it is a way of making effective and loving use of our present ones. The taking on of extra sufferings for the reparation of sin is a special vocation that is to be sought only under the direction of a spiritual director.

When we offer our present sufferings we share in the sufferings of Christ. This is a powerful way to make God's mercy present. Saint Paul had the desire "to know him and the power of his resurrection and the sharing of his sufferings by being conformed to his death if somehow I may attain the resurrection from the dead" (Phil 3:10-11).

Paul desired to be baptized in the Lord's mercy, and he was. He rejoiced in his sufferings for the sake of the Church (cf. Col 1:24). He considered it his special privilege not only to believe in Christ but to suffer for Him (cf. Phil 1:29).

Saint Paul teaches that within suffering are the graces we need: "God is faithful and will not let you be tried beyond your strength; but with the trial he will also provide a way out, so that you will be able to bear it" (1 Cor 10:13).

Agnes Sanford, a women with the gift of healing, teaches the same lesson in her book, *The Healing Power of the Bible* (Philadelphia: Trumpet Books, 1969): "If we can look at the very thing that plagues us, we will think and believe that it can be turned into a source of healing. Then it will be a tool of power, a stepping stone instead of a stumbling block."

The scriptural foundation that we should accept and embrace the source of our suffering is found in Numbers 21:4-9 and is used in the Liturgy for the Feast of the Triumph of the Cross. This text which the Church gives us describes how those who were afflicted by the poisonous bite of the fiery serpents were cured. The Lord told Moses to make an image of the serpent and mount it on a pole. Those who looked at it would recover. In the Gospel reading for the feast, taken from John 3:13-17, Jesus applies this remedy to those who look at Him: "Just as Moses lifted up the serpent in the desert, so must the Son of man be lifted up, that all who believe in him may have eternal life."

Saint John shows how this is fulfilled when Jesus is lifted up on the Cross, and quotes Zechariah 12:10 (also quoted in Rev 1:7): "They shall look on him whom they have pierced." Saint John records this "so that you may believe" (John 19:35).

As we "look to Jesus, the pioneer and perfecter of our faith" (Heb 12:2), we are healed. Like Saint Thomas who put his hand into the pierced side of Jesus, we too cry out, "My Lord and my God!" (John 20:28).

When we unite our sufferings with the pierced and risen Savior, lifted up for our salvation, we, too, in and through Him, become channels of mercy to others. The very source of our pain and suffering becomes a source of mercy, healing, and salvation because Christ acts through His Body, the Church. Your suffering and my suffering bring His saving love, His mercy, to those in need.

Suffering is precious; don't waste it! Suffering is the very way of mercy that the Father chose for His Son. It is the way Jesus embraced for the joy that lay ahead (cf. Heb 12:2), the joy of our final and ultimate healing, our salvation.

# 15

## What Is the Source of Baptism in His Mercy?

WHAT IS THE SOURCE of Divine Mercy? The source of Divine Mercy is the blood and water that poured forth from the opened side of Jesus on the Cross.

How powerfully the Lord taught Blessed Faustina to pray each day the renewal of her commitment to offer her sufferings with those of Christ: "O Blood and Water, which gushed forth from the Heart of Jesus as a Fount of mercy for us, I trust in You" (*Diary*, 309). She was baptized in His mercy by her trust.

The blood, the water, and the Spirit are His gifts of mercy and signs of the total gift of Himself in His three-fold baptism. Saint John records the desire Jesus had to accomplish His total gift in the words "I thirst." He then drank of the wine offered to Him on a sponge as the final cup of His celebration of the new Passover begun the evening before. Then He said, "It is finished" (John 19:30).

He drank the cup the Father offered to Him in the Garden of Olives. He finished the task the Father asked of Him. Then a soldier pierced His side and out flowed the last of His blood and water, the outpouring of His merciful love for us.

Jesus told His Apostles that He would drink of the cup and be baptized in the bath of pain (cf. Matt 20:22;

Mark 10:38). It is this cup of His blood that He offered at the Last Supper as the blood of the New Covenant. He told His disciples to drink it in "remembrance of me" (1 Cor 12:25; see also Matt 26:27; Mark 14:23; Luke 22:20). It is the same cup of His blood that He offers to you and to me in the celebration of each Eucharist, for the forgiveness of sin.

By His blood our sins are cleansed (cf. Heb 9:14) and only by the shedding of His blood do we have forgiveness of our sins (cf. Heb 9:22). The blood of Christ is the source of mercy for us and for the whole world. The blood of Christ truly baptizes us in His mercy.

In Saint Paul's Letter to Timothy, our salvation is described as a gift of God's mercy, washing us and renewing us in the Holy Spirit poured out upon us through Jesus Christ (3:5-8). Mercy can be pictured as the Spirit of Love poured through the pierced Heart of Jesus, gushing forth as blood and water.

The Merciful Jesus is also pictured as the Lamb of God who is pierced and yet lives, by whose blood the elect have been washed clean and given their victory. It is to the wedding feast of this Lamb that we are called in heaven. And we, the Church, are the Bride of the Lamb (cf. Rev 5:6; 7:14; 12:11).

The cup, the pierced Heart, and the Lamb all speak of mercy from the blood of Christ. Because of our sinfulness, misery, hunger, thirst, and sickness, we can turn to the blood of Jesus and receive mercy. When feeling "dirty" and guilty, we can bathe in the fountain of mercy, the blood and water that flow from the pierced Heart of Jesus, and be cleansed of our sins in the Sacrament of Reconciliation.

When thirsty and longing for peace, joy, and love, we can drink the cup offered us and be baptized in His mercy. When miserable, tired, and lonely, we can hide and rest in the Merciful Heart of Jesus. He said, "Come to me, all who labor and are heavy laden, and I will give you rest. Take my yoke upon you, and learn from me; for I am gentle and lowly of heart, and you will find rest for your souls. For my yoke is easy and my burden light" (Matt 11:28-30).

When we are anxious, tense, and under attack, we can pray, "O Blood and Water which gushed forth from the Heart of Jesus as a fount of mercy for us, I trust in You" over and over again until we are baptized in His mercy and experience peace, joy, and love.

When we feel our human condition, when we are overburdened, weak, and powerless or useless, we can go to the Blessed Sacrament and be irradiated by the rays of mercy and be renewed. Or we can place ourselves in silent presence before the image of the Merciful Savior and be irradiated by the rays of blood and water emanating from His Merciful Heart. As we gaze upon the source of all mercy we will be strengthened.

If you need and want God's mercy, then go to the source of it, the blood and water that gushed forth from the pierced Merciful Heart of Jesus. Go with trust and humility and be baptized in His mercy.

The source of all mercy is present in the Eucharist. During Mass, by a miracle of mercy, Mercy itself is made present. We are washed anew by the blood of the Lamb as we celebrate His wedding feast and receive Him in Communion. We are offered the cup of the New Covenant for the forgiveness of our sins. The presence of the pierced,

Merciful Heart is our refuge and our strength. Each Holy Eucharist brings us ever more into the fullness of our initiation into Christ (cf. *Presbyterorum Ordinis*). In the celebration of the Eucharist we not only proclaim the death of the Lord until He comes, but we also proclaim our own death and celebrate our new life in Christ. By our participation in the Eucharist we are baptized in the blood of the Lord, dying with Him that we may rise with Him. This is being baptized in His mercy. In Holy Communion we receive mercy itself and become what we eat, living Eucharist, radiating His mercy. The more we receive mercy with ever greater trust and humility, the more we are transformed by Mercy into mercy and the more we can live baptized in His mercy.

# 16

## I Need to Live Baptized in Mercy, Today

NORMALLY, as I begin each day with prayer, I pray for the grace to be baptized more fully in the mercy of Jesus. I entrust myself to Mary, the Mother of Mercy, asking her to place me in the Merciful Heart of her Son, Jesus. In response to the Lord's desire that we ask, I cry out for mercy to Mercy itself because I know I need mercy. My prayer is simple and all–embracing. I share a sample of my prayer with you so you too can cry out for the mercy of the Lord. You should particularize your prayer to your situation and circumstances.

Lord, I need Your mercy. I need to live baptized in Your mercy, Lord. I need Your mercy to live the way you want me to live, without sin, without fear or anxiety, without self-concern, without depression, to be an apostle of Your mercy, and in total trust. Help me to receive Your mercy so that I may be immersed in it, baptized in Your mercy.

I need to be baptized in Your mercy to experience it, to know it and to be a witness of Your mercy, to be an apostle of Your mercy, to carry out the mission of making Your mercy present.

If You don't baptize me in Your mercy, how can I know, love, and serve Your merciful will and carry out Your plan to have mercy on all (cf. Rom 11:32)? I can't give what I don't have. I need Your mercy to give away to others. I need to know Your mercy in order to tell others. I need to be baptized in Your mercy in order to do all Your marvelous desires and commands:

· To proclaim Your mercy

· To practice Your mercy

· To be merciful as Your Father is merciful (cf. Luke 6:36)

· To offer my sufferings and the sufferings of others with peace, joy, and love

· To make Your Kingdom present as an apostle of Your mercy

· To glorify Your mercy and bring others to glorify it

· To write about Your mercy

· To forgive others as You forgive

· To be a channel of Your mercy to those in sin and misery as an ambassador of reconciliation (cf. 2 Cor 5)

· To offer Your sacrifice of mercy in atonement for my sins and those of the whole world, and

· To TRUST in You!

Lord, I ask for the grace to live today in the very source of all mercy, to live in Your pierced, Merciful Heart. Help me to come to Your Heart, carrying Your yoke, learning from Your mercy, and resting in the source of all mercy. Let me live today in the radiance of the rays of Your mercy, Your blood and water which gushed forth as a fountain of mercy for us. Let me live baptized in Your mercy, today, embracing all that makes up this day with peace, joy, and love.

Mary, my mother, since you are Mother of Jesus and Mother of Mercy, I entrust myself to you anew today so that you would take me to the Cross of your Son, Jesus, to the source of all mercy, to the pierced Heart of Jesus. Place me in His Merciful Heart and keep me there today, resting in Him. Instruct my guardian angel to keep me centered in the Heart of Jesus, focused on Him alone. Mary, you who were the first to be baptized in His mercy at the Cross, ask for that grace for me, that I may live baptized in His mercy today.

Lord, baptize me in Your mercy today so that I may make Your mercy present. "O blood and water which gushed forth from the Heart of Jesus as a Fount of mercy, I trust in You."

# 17

## Blessed Faustina Was
## Baptized in the Lord's Mercy

THE MORE I REFLECTED and prayed over the meaning of being baptized in the Lord's mercy, the more I became aware that Blessed Faustina was immersed in and transformed into God's mercy. Having gathered from her diary a sampling of texts that described her immersion into His mercy, I read them over and over again and I became convinced that the only thing missing was the use of the actual word *baptized*. Blessed Faustina prayed for, received, experienced, understood, practiced, and proclaimed the mercy of God in an extraordinary way. She was baptized in His mercy.

From the texts of her diary, God is seen as Mercy itself, the Divine Mercy, the source of all mercy, overflowing like a fountain. From His pierced Heart mercy pours out in torrents on all who trust in Him with humility. He wants all of us to immerse ourselves and others in His infinite sea of mercy. Further, we see that Blessed Faustina prayed to be transformed into His mercy. The Lord said He wanted mercy to flow through her heart and out to others. He wants to do the same with us; He wants to fill us with such an abundance of mercy that we will radiate His mercy to others.

The following texts sample Blessed Faustina's experience of being baptized in the Lord's mercy. She prayed to be completely transformed into the Lord's mercy, asking that her eyes, her ears, her tongue, her hands, her feet, and her heart would be merciful, and that His mercy would rest upon her:

O Most Holy Trinity! As many times as I breathe, as many times as my heart beats, as many times as my blood pulsates through my body, so many thousand times do I want to glorify Your mercy.

I want to be completely transformed into Your mercy and to be Your living reflection, O Lord. May the greatest of all divine attributes, that of Your unfathomable mercy, pass through my heart and soul to my neighbor.

Help me, O Lord, that my eyes may be merciful, so that I may never suspect or judge from appearances, but look for what is beautiful in my neighbors' souls and come to their rescue.

Help me, that my ears may be merciful, so that I may give heed to my neighbors' needs and not be indifferent to their pains and moanings.

Help me, O Lord, that my tongue may be merciful, so that I should never speak negatively of my neighbor, but have a word of comfort and forgiveness for all.

Help me, O Lord, that my hands may be merciful and filled with good deeds, so that I may do only good to my neighbors and take upon myself the more difficult and toilsome tasks.

Help me, that my feet may be merciful, so that I may hurry to assist my neighbor, overcoming my own fatigue and weariness. My true rest is in the service of my neighbor.

Help me, O Lord, that my heart may be merciful so that I myself may feel all the sufferings of my neighbor. I will refuse my heart to no one. I will be sincere even with those who, I know, will abuse my kindness. And I will lock myself up in the most merciful Heart of Jesus. I will bear my own suffering in silence. May Your mercy, O Lord, rest upon me.

You Yourself command me to exercise the three degrees of mercy. The first: the act of mercy, of whatever kind. The second: the word of mercy—if I cannot carry out a work of mercy, I will assist by my words. The third: prayer—if I cannot show mercy by deeds or words, I can always do so by prayer. My prayer reaches out  even there where I cannot reach out physically.

O my Jesus, transform me into Yourself, for You can do all things. [*Diary*, 163.]

Blessed Faustina saw the rays of mercy come from the Sacred Heart and heard the Lord say that He desired that these rays of mercy should pass through her heart out to the whole world:

Once, the image [of the Merciful Jesus] was being exhibited over the altar during the Corpus Christi procession [June 20, 1935]. When the priest exposed the Blessed Sacrament, and the choir began to sing, the rays from the image pierced the Sacred Host and spread out all over the world. Then I heard these words: "These rays of mercy will pass through you, just as they have passed through this Host, and they will go out through all the world." At these words, profound joy invaded my soul. [*Diary*, 441.]

The Lord described Himself as Mercy itself, expressing a desire to fill souls with so much grace that they would radiate His mercy under the condition that they TRUST HIM: "Tell [all people], My daughter, that I am Love and

Mercy itself. When a soul approaches Me with trust, I fill it with such an abundance of graces that it cannot contain them within itself, but radiates them to other souls" (*Diary*, 1074).

The Lord describes His opened Heart as the fountain and source of all mercy for all:

On the Cross, the fountain of My mercy was opened wide by the lance for all souls—no one have I excluded! [*Diary*, 1182.]

From all My wounds, like from streams, mercy flows for souls, but the wound in My Heart is the fountain of unfathomable mercy. From this fountain spring all graces for souls. The flames of compassion burn Me. I desire greatly to pour them out upon souls. Speak to the whole world about My mercy. [*Diary*, 1190.]

Today the Lord said to me, "I have opened My Heart as a living fountain of mercy. Let all souls draw life from it. Let them approach this sea of mercy with great trust. Sinners will attain justification, and the just will be confirmed in good. Whoever places his trust (115) in My mercy will be filled with My divine peace at the hour of death." [*Diary*, 1520.]

Today the Lord said to me, "Daughter, when you go to confession, to this fountain of My mercy, the Blood and Water which came forth from My Heart always flow down upon your soul and ennoble it. Every time you go to confession, immerse yourself entirely in My mercy, with great trust, so that I may pour the bounty of My grace upon your soul. When you approach the confessional, know this, that I Myself am waiting there for you. I am only hidden by the priest, but I myself act in your soul. Here the misery of the soul meets the God of mercy. Tell souls that from this fount of mercy (7) souls draw graces solely with the vessel of trust. If their trust is great, there is no limit to My generosity. The torrents of grace inundate humble souls. The proud remain always in poverty and misery, because My grace turns away from them to humble souls." [*Diary*, 1602.]

My daughter, know that My Heart is mercy itself. From this sea of mercy, graces flow out upon the whole world. No soul that has approached Me has ever gone away unconsoled. All misery gets buried in the depths of My mercy, and every saving and sanctifying grace flows from this fountain. My daughter, I desire that your heart be an abiding place of My mercy. I desire that this mercy flow out upon the whole world through your heart. Let no one who approaches you go away without that trust in My mercy which I so ardently desire for souls. [*Diary*, 1777.]

The Lord used the word "immerse" in describing our response to His mercy. "Immerse yourself and others in My mercy." These words are another way of saying, "Be baptized in My mercy."

In the great novena in preparation for the Feast of Divine Mercy, the Lord told Blessed Faustina to immerse various groups of souls into His mercy each day, to bring them to the fountain of mercy:

Novena to The Divine Mercy which Jesus instructed me to write down and make before the Feast of Mercy. It begins on Good Friday:

I desire that during these nine days you bring souls to the fount of My mercy, that they may draw therefrom strength and refreshment and whatever graces they need in the hardships of life and, especially, at the hour of death.

On each day you will bring to My Heart a different group of souls, and you will immerse them in this ocean of My mercy, and I will bring all these souls into the house of My Father. You will do this in this life and in the next. I will deny nothing to any soul whom you will bring to the fount of My mercy. On each day you will beg My Father, on the strength of My bitter Passion, for graces for these souls. [*Diary*, 1209.]

The Lord asked Blessed Faustina to immerse herself in His mercy, especially at the three o'clock, the hour of great mercy:

At three o'clock, implore My mercy, especially for sinners; and, if only for a brief moment immerse yourself in My Passion, particularly in My abandonment at the moment of agony. This is the hour of great mercy for the whole world. I will allow you to enter into My mortal sorrow. In this hour, I will refuse nothing to the soul that makes a request of Me in virtue of My Passion.... [*Diary*, 1320.]

This firm resolution to become a saint is extremely pleasing to Me. I bless your efforts and will give you opportunities to sanctify yourself. Be watchful that you lose no opportunity that My providence offers you for sanctification. If you do not succeed in taking advantage of an opportunity, do not lose your peace, but humble yourself profoundly before Me and with great trust, immerse yourself completely in My mercy. In this way you gain more than you have lost, because more favor is granted to a humble soul than the soul itself asks for.... [*Diary*, 1361.]

I remind you, My daughter, that as often as you hear the clock strike the third hour, immerse yourself completely in My mercy, adoring and glorifying it; invoke its omnipotence for the whole world, and particularly for poor sinners; for at that moment mercy was opened wide for every (145) soul. In this hour you can obtain everything for yourself and for others for the asking; it was the hour of grace for the whole world—mercy triumphed over justice. [*Diary*, 1572.]

The necessary condition on our part to be immersed, to be baptized in His mercy, is to TRUST Him. We hear this call to trust in the texts quoted above (1074, 1520, 1602) and again in the expression of His desire: "If only souls would trust."

> Today, in the course of a long conversation, the Lord said to me, "How very much I desire the salvation of souls! My dearest secretary, write that I want to pour out My divine life into human souls and to sanctify them… if only they would trust in My mercy. The very inner depths of My being are filled to overflowing with mercy, and it is being poured out upon all I have created. My delight is to act in a human soul and to fill it with My mercy (133) and to justify it. My kingdom on earth is My life in the human soul. Write, My secretary, that I Myself am the spiritual guide of souls—and I guide them indirectly through the priest, and lead each one to sanctity by a road known to Me alone." [*Diary*, 1784.]

Yes, Blessed Faustina was immersed in God's mercy, transformed into His mercy, baptized in His mercy. She lived in His mercy with trust. She practiced His mercy in deed, word, and prayer. She offered her sufferings with peace, joy, and love. And the Divine Mercy message and devotion is that we too are to live baptized in His mercy.

How can we become apostles of Divine Mercy like Blessed Faustina? There is only one answer: by being baptized in His mercy and living baptized in His mercy. We need to ask to be transformed completely into His mercy like Blessed Faustina so that God's mercy will flow out through us to others.

# 18

## Mary Is Mother of Mercy

MARY WAS THE FIRST to be baptized in the mercy of the Lord. From the moment of her conception in the womb of her mother, Ann, she was immersed in God's mercy. God's mercy protected her from Original Sin and all personal sin. God Himself placed "enmity" between her and the serpent (cf. Gen 3:15) so that Satan had no hold on her. By the "prevenient grace" that is by God's mercy drawn from Christ's passion, death, and resurrection, she was immersed in Divine Mercy by the Eternal Spirit. Mary was baptized in God's mercy in preparation for the moment of Incarnation of the Word of God.

When the angel Gabriel greeted Mary at the announcement of the Father's plan, he greeted her with a new name: *"full of grace"* (John Paul II, *Redemptoris Mater*, n. 8). The angel described her as the favored of God and declared, "The Lord is with you!" (Luke 1:28). The Lord, who is mercy itself (cf. *Diary*, 1074) is with Mary. She is declared baptized in His mercy.

At the wedding feast at Cana, Mary noticed the lack of wine and told her Son about it. But in a mystic way, she also declared that we, His people, do not have the wine of the Spirit and have not yet received His mercy. The abundance (about 120 gallons) of the new wine provided by Jesus in response to Mary's direction to the servants, "Do whatever he tells you" (John 2:5), is a foreshadowing of the abundance of God's mercy poured out on Calvary.

On Calvary, Mary stood at the Cross of Jesus in silence, offering her Son to the Father and receiving His mercy. The water and the blood poured out from the pierced side of Jesus as a fount of mercy for us (cf. John 19:30-37). Mary received the flood of mercy like a great reservoir, and she holds it for us because she is the Mother of Mercy.

Pope John Paul II, in the section "Mother of Mercy" in *Dives in Misericordia,* describes Mary as receiving God's mercy in a remarkable and exceptional way. She shared in the revelation of that mercy by the sacrifice of her heart. *"No one has experienced to the same degree as the Mother of the Crucified One* the mystery of the Cross. . ."* (n. 9). It could be said that she suffered by compassion what Jesus suffered in His passion.

The Holy Father says that because of her maternal heart, Mary is especially suited to share in the revelation of God's mercy "from generation to generation" (Luke 1:50). She is Mother of Mercy, meaning that she is both mother of the Merciful God and also the Mother of God (Theotokos), of Mercy. "She who has the fullest knowledge of the mystery of God's mercy. . . as *the one* who experienced mercy *in an exceptional way,* . . . in an equally exceptional way 'merits' that mercy . . . particularly at the foot of the Cross of her Son" and brings "close to people that love [mercy] which He had come to reveal" (ibid.).

The Holy Father concludes this section on Mary by quoting the Second Vatican Council which explained that Mary continues her maternal role without interruption in heaven and with love cares for the brethren of her Son still on the earthly journey (cf. *Lumen Gentium,* n. 62).

Mary, the Mother of Mercy, herself fully immersed in God's mercy, baptized in His mercy, is also the mediatrix of mercy. She continues to dispense the infinite mercies of God poured out for us on the Cross of her Son. Like a great reservoir, like a sea without limits, she holds the mercies of God in store for us. This mercy is available for the asking. We pray to her because God chose her to be the Mother of Mercy—the Mother of the Merciful God and the Merciful Mother of God, who is Mercy itself—the Divine Mercy.

Mary, you are the Mother of Mercy. Immerse me in that mercy. Baptize me in that mercy. I entrust myself to you so that you would accomplish the will of God in me, that I would be fully baptized in the mercy of your Son. I renew my consecration to you so that I may live baptized in mercy. I place myself into your Immaculate Heart so that you would place me in the Merciful Heart of your Son, Jesus, and keep me there.

Mary, Mother of Jesus and Mother of Mercy, since Jesus from the Cross gave you to me, I take you as my own. And since Jesus gave me to you, take me as your own. Make me docile like Jesus on the Cross, obedient to the Father, trusting in humility and in love. Mary, my mother, in imitation of the Father, who gave his Son to you, I too give my all to you; to you I entrust all that I am, all that I have, and all that I do. Help me to surrender ever more fully to the Spirit. Lead me deeper into the Mystery of the Cross, the Cenacle and the fullness of Church. As you formed the Heart of Jesus by the Spirit, form my heart to be the throne of Jesus in His glorious coming.

## 19

## Mary, the Baptizer in Her Son's Mercy

WHAT DOES OUR MERCIFUL MOTHER actually do? Does she merely pray, asking her Son for mercy, or does she actually do something else? Yes, she does something very effective. She plunges us into the Lord's mercy. Or to use the word derived from the Greek, she baptizes us in His mercy.

Mary is uniquely the baptizer in the Lord's mercy just as she is uniquely the Mother of Mercy in giving birth to Jesus. Now, in God's plan, she does the next most merciful thing: she immerses us into Divine Mercy itself. As Mother Most Merciful she bathes us in the mercy of her Son so that we would be washed clean and healed. As Mother she forms us into the very image of Jesus. She forms us into icons of mercy.

Mary, as Mother of Mercy, is most united to this role of baptizer into the Lord's mercy. At the Cross of her Son, she received mercy in a unique and extraordinary way, experienced it like no other person and came to know and understand it in a profound way. She "merited" it and shared in revealing it "singularly and exceptionally by her heart as the Mother of Jesus." Then at the Cross, by the final commission of her dying Son, she became our Mother of Mercy. How magnificently the Lord prepared Mary to be Mother of Mercy and baptizer in His mercy (cf. *Dives in Misericordia*, n. 9.)

Now Mary as Mother of Mercy responds to our greatest need, our desperate need of God's mercy. She now plunges us into God's mercy when we turn to her as our Merciful Mother, entrusting our lives to her. When we turn to her with our whole hearts and pray to her she baptizes us in the Lord's mercy. She immerses us in His mercy for the forgiveness of our sins, for our salvation, for compassion in our misery, for strength when attacked, for health in our sicknesses, for perseverance in good works, for encouragement in our daily journey, for peace, joy, and love in the midst of our suffering, and for hope and trust in all circumstances.

When Mary, our Merciful Mother, says "Jesus, mercy!" she not only prays for mercy—she "does" mercy! She baptizes us in the mercy of Her Son. Jesus, mercy!

# 20

## How Do I Live Baptized in His Mercy?

MY GREATEST NEED is to live baptized in the Lord's mercy. But how do I live in it? I know that I am baptized in His mercy, but the real issue for me is to live in His mercy, and be ever more immersed in that ocean of mercy.

I am becoming more and more convinced that TRUST is the KEY. Trust in the Lord and in His mercy is the key that opens the floodgates of His mercy and allows the mercy of God to flood us in torrents. Trust is an act of the will declaring that the Lord is God. He loves me and He saves me. He cares for me. Trust is an act of our free will which gives the Lord permission to act freely according to His will without violating our free will. Our trust gives God the freedom to act mercifully. By our trust God can fulfill His plan and desire "to have mercy on all" (Rom 11:32). Trust is the key to receiving mercy. Trust is the key to being merciful like our Father in heaven. Trust is the key to glorifying His mercy. Trust is the key to the Divine Mercy message and devotion as revealed to Blessed Faustina. The short prayer of trust which Jesus asked to be signed at the bottom of the image of Divine Mercy is the summary of how we are to live baptized in His mercy: "Jesus, I trust in You!"

That says it all. Our trust in Jesus keeps us immersed in His mercy. As we repeat from our hearts "Jesus, I trust in You!" we grow in trust and are immersed deeper and deeper into His mercy, and it flows out to others. The more we trust the more we are baptized in His mercy. Trust baptizes us in His mercy.

The essential point about being baptized in God's mercy is that God is Mercy itself. It begins with Him and ends with Him. In order to fulfill the Lord's command that we "be merciful even as our Father is merciful" (Luke 6:36), we need to receive His mercy and be immersed in it so that His mercy can flow out to our neighbor and return to Him with thanks and glory. On our part the essential condition to receive His mercy and let it flow and return to God is TRUST.

I have come to understand that trust is a mystery of our relationship with the Lord. But how can we grow in trust? There are a variety of ways to grow in trust. Let me share with you some of these ways to trust and live baptized in His mercy:

· Abide in the Merciful Heart of Jesus as your resting place and your refuge. The pierced Heart of Jesus is the source of all mercy.

· Place yourself under the fountain of blood and water gushing forth from the pierced side of Jesus like rays of red and pale light. Live in the radiance of these rays of mercy.

· Place yourself in the Sorrowful and Immaculate Heart of Mary, the Mother of Mercy, so that she can place you in the very center of the Merciful Heart of Jesus in the Heart of the heavenly Father. Invite Mary to baptize you in the Lord's mercy.

· Renew your consecration to Mary each day.

· Be present to the Lord with your heart in the Immaculate Heart of Mary, trusting and rejoicing.

· Ask for His mercy. Ask to be baptized in His mercy. Ask to live immersed in His mercy.

· Ask to be transformed into His mercy like Blessed Faustina (cf. *Diary*, 163).

· Live in trust like Mary who was blessed by Elizabeth for her trust: "Blessed is she who trusted that the Lord's words to her would be fulfilled" (Luke 1:45).

· The trust you have shown shall not pass from the memories of men but shall ever remind them of the power of God.

· Ask Mary to teach you how to grow in trust and share in her trust.

· Take time to be irradiated by the eucharistic presence of Mercy itself.

· Let each celebration of the Holy Eucharist and Communion transform you into living Eucharist.

· Live the Eucharist: be holy, be humble, be merciful—like the Lord and like Mary.

· Live Mary's Magnificat, glorifying God's holiness, His mercy, and His humility.

· Live the way of trust taught by Saint Paul: "Rejoice always. Pray without ceasing. In all circumstances give thanks, for this is the will of God in Christ Jesus regarding you all" (1 Thess 5:16-18).

· Offer each moment of your life in peace, joy and love in union with the eucharistic Lord for mercy on all.

· Ask your guardian angel to keep you focused on the Lord and immersed in His mercy.

· Plunge into the infinite ocean of His mercy.

I would like to gather these suggested ways to trust and to live baptized in the Lord's mercy under the three special works of the Holy Spirit—Mercy, Mary, and Eucharist:

Radiate His mercy.
Sing Mary's Magnificat with your life.
Be living Eucharist: be holy, be humble, be merciful.

# PART FOUR

# THE MISSION OF MERCY

# 21

## The Mission of Jesus
## Was to Make Mercy Present

JESUS WAS SENT among us to reveal the heavenly Father's mercy by making His mercy present. Pope John Paul II develops this mission of Jesus in three of his encyclicals. In *Dives in Misericordia* he says: "In and through Christ, God becomes remarkably visible in His mercy" (n. 2). And,

> Through these [His] actions and words Christ makes the Father present among men...*as love and mercy*...[which] is the fundamental proof of His mission as the Messiah. Jesus makes mercy one of the principal *topics of His preaching*....[And] by becoming the incarnation of love, which is seen with special force in the face of suffering, the unfortunate and sinners, [He] makes present and so more fully reveals the Father, who is God "rich in mercy." [*Dives in Misericordia*, n. 3.]

Jesus made the Father's mercy present! The fullness of the revelation of the Father's mercy is revealed by Jesus on the Cross: "In this way redemption involves the revelation in its fullness" (ibid., n. 7). And John Paul II points out the meaning of our response to God's love:

> ... He "so loved the world"—therefore man in the world—that "he gave his only Son, that whoever believes in him shall not perish but have eternal life"

(John 3:16). Believing in the crucified Son means "seeing the Father" (John 14:9), means believing that love is present in the world and that this love is more powerful than any kind of evil. . . . Believing in this love means *believing in mercy*. [Ibid., n. 7.]

Pope John Paul II emphasizes that the mission of Jesus is also the mission of the Church: "Christ's messianic program, the program of mercy, becomes the program of His people, the program of the Church" (ibid., n. 8). The fullest expression of this program of mercy is seen in the death and resurrection of Christ. The Paschal Christ (crucified and risen) is the definitive incarnation of mercy, its "living sign" and its "inexhaustible source" (ibid.).

The summit of Christ's revelation of the Father's mercy on the Cross is at the same time the source of all mercy—His spirit handed over, His blood and water flowing out upon the world as a fountain of mercy for us. He reveals the Father's mercy by immersing us in that mercy. He accomplishes His mission of mercy by baptizing us in His mercy!

In the encyclical on the Holy Spirit, *Dominum et Vivificantem*, Pope John Paul II describes the role of the Holy Spirit in transforming suffering into salvific love, that is into mercy. The Spirit who convinces the world concerning sin also reveals the effect of sin, revealing suffering and pain, and He does something about it. He brings the sin and its resultant suffering and pain to the source of mercy, the Cross, in an outpouring of salvific love (cf. n. 39).

The action of the Holy Spirit enables eternal salvific love to spring forth from suffering (cf. *Dominum et Vivificantem*, n. 40). The Holy Spirit is the fire of love that consumes the sacrifice of Christ and is made present as love (ibid., n. 41). Christ through the Holy Spirit makes suffering the source of mercy!

We, too, can offer our sufferings (cf. Rom 12:1) through the Holy Spirit and like Saint Paul can find our joy in the sufferings we endure for the sake of Christ (cf. John Paul II, *Salvifici Doloris*, n. 1; Col 1:24). We can offer our sufferings with and through Christ to make His mercy present. In the words of Eucharistic Prayer III, the priest prays to the Father that the Holy Spirit "make us an everlasting gift."

By being baptized in His mercy we can make His mercy present to others and so share in the mission of Christ.

In his encyclical on the Church's missionary mandate, *Redemptoris Missio*, Pope John Paul II points out that the mission of Christ is to make the Kingdom of God present (cf. n. 13). Then he shows that the Kingdom of God is fulfilled in Christ who "is the revelation and incarnation of the Father's mercy" (*Redemptoris Missio*, n. 12). "Jesus himself is the 'Good News' of the Kingdom" (ibid., n. 13). The "Good News" is the presence of mercy incarnate among us. Jesus made the Kingdom present by making mercy present.

From these three encyclicals of John Paul II we can say that the mission of Jesus was to make mercy present. He did so not only by His preaching, healing, and forgiving of sin; through the Eternal Spirit He made suffering the source of mercy for all who receive it.

When we receive His mercy by our trust and are baptized in His mercy, we become channels of His mercy to others. In this way we share in and continue the mission of Christ to make the Kingdom of God present, so as to make the mercy of the Father present.

Lord, fill us with Your mercy so that we may be merciful. Baptize us in Your mercy so that we may make Your mercy present.

# 22

# Be Makers of Mercy Present,
# Not Military Police

BE MAKERS OF MERCY PRESENT, *MMP's*. That is what we should be. That is what Jesus asks us to do, to make mercy present. But we so easily and so often find ourselves judging, gossiping, criticizing, condemning, trying to control situations and lives, and trying to put them in order according to our own rules. We end up being military police, *MP's* of others' lives, our families, our work places, and our parishes rather than making mercy present. What makes the difference? The only answer is mercy! Mercy makes the difference.

We are commanded by Jesus to "be merciful even as our heavenly Father" (Luke 6:36). Like Jesus, our mission in life is to make mercy present and believable, and to show it in our own lives. The Church teaches that we make mercy present when we practice the spiritual and the corporal works of mercy, which are gleaned from Sacred Scripture:

THE CORPORAL WORKS OF MERCY

   1. Feed the hungry.

   2. Give drink to the thirsty.

3. Clothe the naked.

4. Shelter the homeless.

5. Visit the imprisoned.

6. Visit the sick.

7. Bury the dead.

THE SPIRITUAL WORKS OF MERCY

1. Admonish sinners.

2. Instruct the uninformed.

3. Counsel the doubtful.

4. Comfort the sorrowful.

5. Bear wrongs patiently.

6. Forgive offenses.

7. Pray for the living and dead.

But what about judgments? Aren't parents, teachers, pastors, and those in authority supposed to judge what is right and what is wrong, what is truth and what is error? Yes, of course we must judge and use our faculties of observation and intelligence, but we are to judge, not to condemn with a self-righteous pride, but rather to have mercy. We are to make mercy present where mercy is needed. We are to bring forgiveness, healing, truth, righteousness, and peace. It is this kind of mercy that Jesus brought into the world and even now pours upon us, so that we may be merciful to others as He has been merciful to us.

Since all that we have is a gift from God, who are we to judge and to boast with self-righteous finger-pointing at others because they are different from us? We should have an attitude of thanksgiving for the gifts we receive those in need with an attitude of compassionate mercy. We can inject God's mercy into every circumstance of our daily routine by turning to the Merciful Lord with trust and thanksgiving.

What can we do if in fact we find ourselves in the midst of judgment and criticism? We can respond with a plea for mercy. We can intercede for mercy, crying out, "Jesus, mercy!" We can extend our plea for mercy by praying the Chaplet of Divine Mercy, and we can bring the situation to Christ in the Holy Eucharist.

There is always something positive we can do when we are tempted to be *MP's*. We can turn to Divine Mercy itself and make mercy present. We can be *MMP's* rather than *MP's*.

# 23

## Blessed Faustina's Mission of Mercy

THE MISSION of Blessed Faustina was MERCY, and the heart of her mission of mercy was to glorify the Lord's mercy. She glorified God's mercy in all her deeds, words, and prayers. In this life and in the next, her mission was to glorify the Divine Mercy (cf. *Diary*, 281, 483, 729, 1242, 1325, 1452, 1553, and 1729). She wanted to be known as a saint who glorified the Merciful Heart of Jesus as the mission of her life:

> O my Jesus, each of Your saints reflects one of Your virtues; I desire to reflect Your compassionate Heart, full of mercy; I want to glorify it. Let Your mercy, O Jesus, be impressed upon my heart and soul like a seal, and this will be my badge in this and the future life. Glorifying Your mercy is the exclusive task of my life. [*Diary*, 1242.]

In compiling a thematic index of her diary, I found a clue to her mission of mercy. Her desire was to be a saint, not just an ordinary saint but a special canonized saint with a capital "S." Her diary records more than a dozen times her expression of that desire (cf. *Diary*, 1326, 1333, 1361, 1362, 1372, 1410, 1571, 1581, 1650).

Her deep longing for union with God alone, to be a saint, made it possible for the Lord to bring her to a unique union with Him (cf. e.g., *Diary*, 707, 1021, 1546, 1631, 1693). This union of her heart with the Heart of the Lord Jesus (cf.

e.g., *Diary*, 703, 742, 1021, 1024, 1669) is the foundation of her mission of mercy.

Her desire to be a saint had the basic characteristic of "humble obedience to the will of God," the characteristic of Jesus, of Mary, of Joseph, and of all the saints. The unique element in Blessed Faustina's life and mission was her total immersion in God's mercy. She was baptized in His mercy, as we reflected on in Part III.

Her response to God's mercy was explosive! I would call it dynamite, TNT (Trinitrotoluene), *Trust 'n Thanksgiving*.

Her TRUST in God's mercy was an echo of the Blessed Mother's trust that was blessed by Saint Elizabeth: "Blessed are you who believed that what was spoken to you by the Lord would be fulfilled" (Luke 1:45).

The trust of Blessed Faustina was beyond all abandonment (cf. *Diary*, 1337, 1489, 1679). It was part of her mission to encourage souls to trust in God (cf. *Diary*, 1182, 1452, 1690).

THANKSGIVING was her special way of glorifying God's mercy. She desired that her whole life would be one act of thanksgiving to God (cf. *Diary*, 1285); it was a eucharistic way of life (cf. *Diary*, 1670). She described seven days of continuous thanksgiving (cf. *Diary*, 1367-1369) as the high point of her life of thanksgiving.

Blessed Faustina also glorified God's mercy and carried out her mission by:

· Interceding for souls of the living, the dying, and the dead. She did this both by praying for and by offering her sufferings for souls. Her great concern was for sinners, that they would turn with trust to the mercy of the Lord.

· Works of mercy by deeds, words, and prayer (cf. *Diary*, 742).

· Promotion of the Divine Mercy message and devotion by the writing of her diary for the benefit of souls (cf. *Diary*, 895, 1142, 1146, 1317, 1471).

The heart of the mission of Blessed Faustina was proclaiming God's mercy. How beautifully our Lord called her by various titles describing her mission:

· Witness of His mercy (cf. *Diary*, 164, 400, 417, 689, 699, 848, 1074)

· Apostle of His mercy (cf. *Diary*, 1142, 1588)

· Secretary of His mercy (cf. *Diary*, 965, 1273, 1275, 1605, 1784)

· His instrument (cf. *Diary*, 645)

· Dispenser (cf. *Diary*, 31, 580), mediator, and intercessor of His mercy (cf. *Diary*, 438, 441, 599).

He topped the list of special titles by calling her a Saint (cf. *Diary*, 1571, 1650).

In this life and in the next, she continues her mission of glorifying the Divine Mercy.

# 24

## Mercy: The Heart of the Mass

THE EUCHARISTIC LITURGY, the Mass, is the MERCY of God remembered, asked for, made present, received, and acknowledged with thanksgiving. It is a celebration of God's mercy from the beginning to the end.

In the Mass mercy is made present in Christ Jesus, made present as *Mercy Incarnate.*

In the Old Testament the mercy of God is the foundation of God's revelation to the Jewish people. The Lord God reveals his love as mercy: tender, compassionate, always faithful, saving, and bringing true peace. This merciful love of God is the basis of the covenant, i.e., committed love. God commits himself, "I am your God and you are my people." This covenant was ratified by circumcision and sealed by a sacrificial banquet.

In the New Covenant mercy takes on a further dimension, readiness to forgive. John Paul II calls this dimension "the divine dimension of redemption." In the Paschal Mystery "redemption involves the revelation of mercy in its fullness" (*Dives in Misericordia,* n. 7). Jesus made this dimension of forgiveness integral to the celebration of the Eucharist: "Drink from it [this cup], all of you, for this is my blood of the covenant, which will be shed on behalf of many for the forgiveness of sins" (Matt 26:27-28).

To understand the full meaning of the Mass, Pope John Paul II points out in his first encyclical, *Redemptor Hominis* (cf. n. 20), that we must grasp three fundamental dimensions of the Eucharist. It is a Sacrament of *presence,* a Sacrament of *sacrifice,* and a Sacrament of *communion.*

By the power of the Holy Spirit and the priestly words of institution, the celebrant fulfills the command of Jesus on the night before He died, "Do this in memory of me" (Luke 22:19). The bread and wine become the Body and Blood of our Lord Jesus Christ. The Lord Jesus, who suffered, died and rose from the dead, is now present. The power of His sacrifice of mercy that satisfied all justice is present. Mercy Incarnate is present so that we may be transformed more fully into His Body by communion. In this way we can be merciful as our heavenly Father is merciful (cf. Luke 6:36).

In the Mass the Holy Spirit is invoked twice: first, upon the gifts of bread and wine in order that they may become the Body and Blood of Christ; and second, upon us, the assembly, who partake of the Body and Blood of Christ so that we may become "one body, one spirit in Christ" (Eucharistic Prayer III). At the Mass, Christ is made present under the appearances of bread and wine so that He may be made present to the world in and through us.

The Mass Is a Presence, a Sacrifice,

and a Communion of Mercy

Mercy itself, Jesus Christ, is made present so that mercy may be made present to the world. The Eucharist is God's sacrificial gift of mercy, offered in atonement for our sins and those of the whole world (cf. 1 John 2:2); in receiving it in Holy Communion, we are strengthened and consoled by the Lord who is Mercy itself.

## Mercy in the Opening Rites of the Liturgy of the Eucharist

· The Sign of the Cross begins the Liturgy and points to the source of all mercy.

· The Greeting of the priest is a welcome in the name of God's merciful love.

· The Penitential Rite leads us to repent of our sins and ask for mercy. Each of the penitential forms cries out for mercy: "Lord, have mercy. Christ, have mercy. Lord, have mercy." And then the priest prays: "May almighty God have mercy on us, forgive us our sins, and bring us to everlasting life." The people respond "Amen."

· The priest then leads us in giving glory to God (in the Gloria) for his mercy, for sending Jesus Christ as the sacrificial Lamb of God to take away the sin of the world.

· Frequently, the Opening Prayer is addressed to God the Father as the God of Mercy, who has poured out His love for us in Christ Jesus!

The Church is conscious of our sinfulness and our human condition and our need for mercy! Therefore, at each Liturgy, we ask for mercy over and over again. Only God's mercy is the answer.

## The Liturgy of the Word

The Old Testament readings used during Mass are records of God's mercy on His chosen people. Israel was the people of the covenant with God, a covenant Israel broke many times. But God in His mercy responded when the Israelites appealed to His mercy (cf. *Dives in Misericordia*, n. 4).

The Responsorial Psalm is often a cry for mercy. The psalmist sings of the Lord of love, of tenderness, of mercy, and of fidelity. "Mercy is the content of intimacy with their Lord, the content of the dialogue with him" (ibid.).

In the New Testament readings, "'God, who is rich in mercy' (Eph 2:4) is the one whom Jesus Christ revealed to us as *Father*. It is His very Son who revealed Him and made Him visible in Himself" (*Dives in Misericordia*, n. 1). This opening sentence of Pope John Paul II's encyclical *Dives in Misericordia* sums up the message of the New Covenant in Jesus Christ who is, in the words of the Holy Father, mercy visible, personified, and incarnate (ibid., nn. 2, 8). Jesus makes mercy present, models it, and proclaims it by His actions and words. The merciful shall obtain mercy (cf. Matt 5:7).

Before the proclamation of the Gospel the priest prays for mercy in order to be purified: "Almighty God, cleanse my heart and lips that I may worthily proclaim your gospel." After the Gospel the priest says quietly, "May the words of the gospel wipe away our sins." The very proclamation of the Gospel is a work of mercy that cleanses us of our sins.

The homily is a proclamation and a celebration of God's mercy revealed in Jesus Christ. The message and reality of His merciful love is made present to the assembly so they too may know and experience His mercy. The "now" word is MERCY, present in its saving power, in the gathering in the name of the Lord and in His Sacraments.

The profession of the Creed is a profession in the God of mercy: the Father creating, the Son redeeming, and the Holy Spirit sanctifying.

The General Intercessions (Prayer of the Faithful) are a plea for mercy; "Lord, hear our prayer" or "Lord, have mercy." They are a plea for mercy on us and on the whole Church and world.

## THE LITURGY OF THE EUCHARIST

The Preparation of the Gifts: The bread and wine are offered to the Lord with a prayer acknowledging that it is through His goodness, His mercy, that we have these gifts to offer.

The Preface: Each preface begins with the dialogue that expresses thanks to the Father, the all-powerful and ever-living God, for the love He gives us in Christ our Lord. The various prefaces for the seasons of the Church year and feast days are preambles to the Eucharistic Prayer that describe the Father's merciful love.

The Sanctus: The Thrice-Holy God is praised for sending his Son, Mercy incarnate.

The Eucharistic Prayer: The eucharistic prayers of the Roman Rite are a threefold proclamation of mercy: mercy as the presence of love, mercy as the sacrifice of love, and mercy as the union of love (cf. *Redemptor Hominis,* n. 20; *Dives in Misericordia,* n. 13).

The eucharistic prayers are *proclamations* of mercy, a *celebration* of God's mercy, and an *offering* of the Merciful One to the Father. The celebrant pleads for mercy on us and on the whole world. The eucharistic prayers make it clear that all the priestly people *proclaim, celebrate,* and *offer* by virtue of their baptism. The priest, by virtue of holy orders, presides and confects the Eucharist by the power of the Holy Spirit.

Eucharistic Prayers I, II, III, and IV invoke the Holy Spirit upon the gifts of bread and wine that they may become the Body and Blood of Christ. In the very words of the consecration of the cup, the mercy of God is proclaimed: "Take this, all of you, and drink from it: this is the cup of my blood, the blood of the new and everlasting covenant. It will be shed for you and for all so that sins may be forgiven."

The readiness to forgive sins is the great new dimension of New Covenant mercy.

The eucharistic prayers recall the great act of mercy, the passion, death, resurrection, and ascension of Jesus into glory. We then return the gift of the Merciful Jesus to the Father in thanksgiving (the meaning of the word *eucharist* in the Greek language).

The priest continues to pray, invoking the Holy Spirit a second time, that the people may "be filled with every grace and blessing" (I); "be brought together in unity by the Holy Spirit" (II); "may be filled with his Holy Spirit and become one body, one spirit in Christ" (III); be gathered "by your Holy Spirit . . . into the one body of Christ, a living sacrifice of praise" (IV). These are the invocations to the Holy Spirit, the Spirit of Mercy, asking that we, the People of God, truly will become the Mystical Body of Christ, living Eucharist!

In each of the eucharistic prayers the priest invokes the mercy of God on us sinners: "Though we are sinners, we trust in Your mercy and love. Do not consider what we truly deserve, but grant us Your forgiveness" (I). "Have mercy on us all; make us worthy to share eternal life with Mary. . ." (II). "In mercy and love unite all Your children wherever they may be" (III). "Father, in Your mercy grant also to us, Your children, to enter into our heavenly inheritance. . ." (IV).

The Communion Rite: The Lord's Prayer is a plea for mercy! We ask for our daily bread, for all our spiritual and material needs. We ask for forgiveness of our sins as we forgive others. We ask to be protected in temptation and delivered from evil. We ask for God's mercy!

In the prayer that follows we again ask for mercy to deliver us from evil and grant us peace. We ask for mercy as a "prevenient" grace, a grace in advance. "In Your mercy keep us free from sin and protect us from all anxiety as we wait in joyful hope for the coming of our Savior, Jesus Christ."

In the Sign of Peace we ask for God's mercy expressed as the peace and forgiveness that we share with one another.

At the Breaking of the Bread we cry, "Lamb of God, You take away the sins of the world: have mercy on us. . . . grant us peace."

In preparation for the reception of Holy Communion, the priest lifts up the Body of the Lord, proclaiming Jesus as the Lamb of God, as Mercy itself, who takes away our sins. And the people respond with a prayer for mercy: "Lord, I am not worthy to receive You, but only say the word and I shall be healed."

The MASS is MERCY! From the beginning to the final blessing and dismissal, the mercy of God is proclaimed, offered, received, and celebrated.

The celebrant could rightly dismiss us with the words, "This Eucharist is celebrated, go in the *mercy* of our Lord Jesus Christ!"

# 25

## A New Wave of the Holy Spirit

THERE IS A NEW WAVE of the Holy Spirit coming, a wave of Divine Mercy. We see signs of this new wave in the working of the Holy Spirit. We can "read the signs of the times in the light of the Gospel" (*Lumen Gentium*) and see the Holy Spirit's work through Mary, the Eucharist, and Divine Mercy.

### MARY

The number of reported apparitions of Mary during this past century has accelerated to such an extraordinary degree, especially in the last decade, that even the secular media have taken a look at these events. *Time* and *Life* magazines pictured Mary on their front covers with major articles on her apparitions (Fall 1992). *The Wall Street Journal* had a report on the front page about Mary's prophetic word at Fatima, over seventy years ago, concerning the conversion of Russia. The report of Marian apparitions and messages are so numerous that we would have to be resisting stubbornly not to have heard of at least some of them.

Pope John Paul II has consistently consecrated to Mary each of the nations he has visited. His consecrations culminated in the solemn collegial consecration of all the nations, including Russia, to the Immaculate Heart of Mary. He knelt in St. Peter's Square before the statue of Our Lady of Fatima which the Bishops of Fatima brought on the Solemnity of the Annunciation, 1984, and prayed this significant entrustment of the whole world to Mary. From that day on there can be traced the progressive opening up of the Eastern European bloc and the dissolution of Soviet Communism and the Soviet Union itself. Afterwards the Holy Father proclaimed the Marian year in preparation for the coming millennium and published an encyclical on Mary, *Redemptoris Mater.*

Centers and conferences on Mary have sprung up across the world. The Marian Movement of Priests has touched thousands of priests and millions of lay faithful around the world. Marian devotions and the praying of the Rosary are being revived.

The year 1992 (February 18) marked the twenty-fifth anniversary of the Duquesne weekend that sparked the worldwide Catholic charismatic renewal. The weekend began with a meditation on Mary. The new wave of the Holy Spirit is bringing about the triumph of the Immaculate Heart prophesied by Mary at Fatima in 1917.

## EUCHARIST

There is a renewal of eucharistic adoration. Pope John Paul II has established daily eucharistic adoration of the Blessed Sacrament in St. Peter's Basilica. There is a growing desire among the faithful for eucharistic adoration. In South Korea, under the direction of Fr. Gerald Farrell, M.M., over one hundred parishes now have perpetual adoration. The work of Fr. Martin Lucia to bring about perpetual adoration of the Blessed Sacrament in parish churches is known all over the world.

In the diary of Blessed Faustina the Eucharist has a major role in the message of and devotion to the Merciful Savior. On numerous occasions she saw the Eucharist with the rays of mercy streaming from it.

The Marian apparitions in Akita, Japan, began with the radiance of the Eucharist as Sister Agnes Sagawa opened the tabernacle for eucharistic adoration. This happened three days in a row.

I consider it significant that the sovereign action of God, baptizing the students at the Duquesne weekend on Saturday night (February 1967), was before the Blessed Sacrament.

The new wave of the Holy Spirit is bringing about a renewed focus on the Eucharist. The sign of this renewal may well be the radiance of the Eucharist that Sister Agnes witnessed in Akita.

I also consider it significant that I experienced the baptism in the Holy Spirit in front of the Blessed Sacrament, some time after midnight on the Feast of All Saints in 1968. I had been at a prayer meeting at St. Mary's Newman Center, Ann Arbor, Michigan, and afterwards asked to be prayed with for the baptism in the Spirit. When a few of the young people prayed over me, I didn't experience any obvious manifestation of the Spirit other than peace. But when I reached home in Windsor, Ontario, and visited the little chapel over the main entrance of Assumption University to thank the Lord in the Blessed Sacrament, I began to laugh and to cry at the same time, fully aware of the Lord's presence in my time of darkness.

He was with me all the time and I heard the word within my heart, "Now can you tell my people about my love and compassion." In retrospect, I realize that was my commission to proclaim God's mercy—and it happened before the eucharistic presence.

## DIVINE MERCY

The Divine Mercy message and devotion has spread around the world. This is the work of the Holy Spirit, the Spirit of Mercy.

Our Holy Father John Paul II, in his encyclical *Dives in Misericordia*, points out how devotion to Divine Mercy has grown: "Many individuals and groups guided by a lively sense of faith are turning, I would say almost spontaneously, to the Mercy of God. They are certainly being moved to do this by Christ himself, who through His Spirit works in human hearts" (n. 2).

Devotion to Divine Mercy is part of the Holy Father's personal life. In 1968, as Bishop of Krakow, he introduced the cause of Blessed Faustina for beatification. On April 10, 1991, he stated that she was instrumental in bringing "the Easter message of the merciful Christ" not only to Poland during the World War II years, but also to the whole world. He reminds us how much we need that message today (cf. *L'Osservatore Romano*, April 15, 1991).

The message of Divine Mercy is that God is Mercy itself and asks for our trust in order that we may receive His mercy and then be merciful to others. This is the heart of the Gospel message. The various vessels of mercy, such as the proposed feast of Divine Mercy, the image of the Merciful Savior, the chaplet of Divine Mercy, the novena to the Divine Mercy, and the three o'clock devotion are reminders of the demands of God's mercy: to trust, to be vessels, to receive His mercy, and to be merciful.

The urgency of this message of mercy, to turn to God's mercy now while it is time for mercy, makes this work of the Holy Spirit both significant and essential.

## The Spirit of Mercy

The Holy Spirit is at work in Mary, in the Eucharist, and in mercy. The Holy Spirit is the spouse of Mary, the Mother of Mercy. Through her the Spirit baptizes us in Divine Mercy.

The Holy Spirit transubstantiates the bread and wine into the Body and Blood of Christ, into the Body and Blood born of Mary, now glorified. This is a miracle of Divine Mercy. It is the holy, humble, merciful presence of Christ among us.

The Holy Spirit is at work in making Christ's mission present. That is, He makes mercy present. We all need God's mercy to make Christ's mission our own mission. We all need to be baptized in the Divine Mercy. This is the work of the Spirit. We all need to be baptized into Divine Mercy to counteract the growing secularization and unrest in the Church, in the world, and in our own lives.

## What Can We Expect?

We can expect a wave of purification prior to the new wave of the Spirit. The Spirit convicts the world of sin, and the world in each of us as well (cf. John 16:8). He is convicting us of sin in order for us to bring our sin to the Cross, the source of salvific love, to mercy (cf. John Paul II, *Dominum et Vivificantem,* n. 28). It is the Spirit's work of mercy to purify us in preparation for the new wave. The time of purification can be seen in various catastrophic events, natural, human, and supernatural. We can expect tribulation, chastisements, signs in the heavens and on earth, and apostasy in the Church, all of which will get worse before they get better. These are apocalyptic times (John Paul II at Fatima, 1982), times of travail.

This pattern of travail is the pattern of the life of Christ our Head. We as members of His Body can expect the same pattern. Born of Mary by the Spirit and led by the Spirit to do the works of the Father, He offered Himself as the Immaculate Victim and an acceptable sacrifice on the Cross. Through the eternal Spirit, He was raised from the dead and now reigns upon the throne of the Father, pouring out that same Spirit on those who believe and trust. This is the pattern Jesus set for us in His threefold baptism in water, the Spirit, and the blood.

We see this pattern around us in the signs of the times: Mary, the Spirit, and travail. The travail of our purification and suffering is the travail of a new birth given us by the great mercy of God (cf. 1 Pet 1:3).

We will see the "new wave" of Mary, Mercy, and Eucharist, a new "MME" generation to replace the old "ME" generation of the past decades. When you see these come to pass, "stand erect, lift up your heads, for your deliverance is at hand" (Luke 21:28). The Spirit is at work in our day:

· Renewing the face of the earth. We see the signs of purification in the travail and in Mary, Mercy, and the Eucharist.

· Revealing the Father's mercy in Christ Jesus.

· Making Divine Mercy present in the world through you and through me, the members of Christ's Body, the Church.

· Baptizing us in Divine Mercy through Mary, the Mother of Mercy.

· Transforming our suffering into salvific love, into mercy.

· Making us into living Eucharist by transforming and offering us to be totally given, holy, humble, and merciful.

· Establishing the Kingdom of Jesus Christ, our Lord.

· Glorifying the Eternal Father.

How Can We Prepare for and Hasten the New Wave of the Spirit?

· Be holy
· Be humble
· Be merciful
· Like Jesus and like Mary.
· Be living Eucharist.
· Live the Magnificat.
· Radiate His mercy and live baptized in His mercy.

What Will the New Wave of the Spirit Bring About?

· The glorious coming of Jesus Christ in a reign of peace and justice, truth and love.

· The new advent described by Pope John Paul II.

· The new Pentecost prayed for by Popes John XXIII and Paul VI.

· The triumph of the Immaculate Heart of Mary and a time of peace described by Mary at Fatima.

· A miracle of mercy.

LET US PRAY

· Come, Holy Spirit, and fill the hearts of the faithful.

· Come, Holy Spirit, by means of the powerful intercession of the Immaculate Heart of Mary, your well-beloved spouse.

· Come, Holy Spirit; baptize us in Divine Mercy through our Mother of Mercy.

· Come, Holy Spirit, in a new wave of mercy.

· Come, Holy Spirit, and renew the face of the earth.

· Come, Holy Spirit, and bring to fulfillment the glorious reign of Jesus Christ our Lord to the

· Glory of God the Father. Amen. Alleluia.

# APPENDIX A

## Spirituality and the Message of Divine Mercy
## as Revealed to Blessed Faustina
## Compared with the Letter to the Hebrews

Systems of Tables:
- A) Letter to the Hebrews Compared with the diary of Blessed Faustina.
- B) The "Let us" exhortations in the Letter to the Hebrews.
- C) The Diary of Blessed Faustina Compared with the Letter to the Hebrews.

A. Letter to the Hebrews Compared with the Diary of Blessed Faustina

| LETTER TO THE HEBREWS | DIARY OF BLESSED FAUSTINA |
| --- | --- |
| 2:17 Christ becomes like His brethren, therefore true Mediator<br>5:9–10 Christ is High Priest<br>7:1–28 | Image—white robe (47)<br>Cenacle (136) |
| 3:1–4:14 Worthy of trust | Jesus, I trust in You! (47)<br>Vessel of trust (1578)<br>Trust receiver (687, 1777) |
| 4:15–5:10 Merciful | "I am Mercy itself" (281, 300, 1074, 1148, 1273, 1739) |

| | |
|---|---|
| Christ's humanity is transformed<br>5:9–10 Perfected<br>7:1–28 Made High Priest<br>8:1–9:28 Glorified<br>    The New Tent<br>    Sacrifice | Image—white robe (47)<br>Jesus at the Cenacle (684)<br>Glorified (777–779)<br>Living Host (1826)<br>My name is Sacrifice (135) |
| Transformed by His<br>4:15–5:10 Obedience<br>8:1–9:28 Reverent plea<br>Passion—Death—<br>    Resurrection<br>Mercy | Obedience (535, 603, 624<br>Bold prayer (873) Chaplet<br>Share in Passion (1032,<br>    1612, 1626)<br>Fire of God's love (745,<br>    778) |
| Christ transforms us<br>9:11–14 We have access<br>    to the Father<br>9:24–28 We have a new<br>    relation with the<br>    Father<br>10:1–18 Sanctified by His<br>    blood, we are given<br>    salvation | Oblation (136)<br>Transconsecrated (137)<br>Transform me (483, 682)<br><br><br><br><br>Feast of Divine Mercy<br>Desire for souls (1032) |
| Christ offers self by the<br>    Eternal Spirit<br>9:14<br>10:19–39 Be generous<br>    Christians<br>10:36–39 Endure<br>Live by faith | Cenacle (684)<br><br><br>Deeds of mercy (742)<br>Seek always God's will<br>    (1667, 1264)<br>Trust (1489, 1584) |

| | |
|---|---|
| 5:11–10:39 Unique value of Christ's sacrifice | Cenacle (684, 765)<br>Eucharistic experience of Passion (616, 914, 1392, 1489, 1670) |
| 11:1–12:13 Faith and endurance<br>11:1–40 Faith of ancestors<br>12:1–13 Necessary endurance<br>12:13 Make the paths straight | TRUST (1488, 1489)<br>Help of saints<br>Humble obedience to God's will (795, 1359)<br>Seek the Lord alone<br>Seek holiness (856, 1145, 1359) |
| 12:14–13:18 The straight path<br>12:14–29 Sanctification<br>13:1–6 Christian attitudes<br>13:7–19 True community | Desire for sanctity (1326)<br>Hospitality, deeds of mercy (1282, 1312)<br>Orthodoxy—obedience, intimacy with Christ, suffering with Christ, sacrament of Church, works of mercy, intercession, daily duties |
| 13:20–21 Conclusion | Turn to God's mercy with trust (300, 1578, 1679, 1690) |

## B. Exhortations

| LETTER TO THE HEBREWS | DIARY OF BLESSED FAUSTINA |
|---|---|
| 4:1 Let us fear, therefore, lest ever any one of you should be wanting. | Pray and suffer for souls, esp. sinners (745, 1426, 1637, 1666, 1777, 1783) |
| 4:10–11 Let us hasten, therefore, to enter into that rest, lest anyone fall in the same model of unfaithfulness. | Take refuge in the Merciful Heart of Jesus (801, 1033, 1287, 1348, 1621, 1629) Desire for souls (72, 648, 679) |
| 4:14 Let us hold fast to the profession [of Jesus 3:11]. | Trust, love (723, 1074, 1784) |
| 4:16 Let us approach, therefore, with accorded right to the throne of grace so we may receive mercy (2:17). | Turn to His mercy now (1035, 1159) Chaplet (848, 1541) Intercession (202, 294, 835, 1582) |
| 6:1 Let us move on to the perfection. . . . | Jesus speaks to striving and perfect souls (1488, 1489) Union of hearts (238, 239, 1754) and desire for union (1121, 1720) |

| | |
|---|---|
| | Transformation (483, 641, 832, 908, 1289, 1564, 1622, 1826) |
| 10:22 Let us approach with a true heart in fullness of faith. . . . | Trust (47, 1273, 274, 1541, 1784)<br>Thanksgiving (1285, 1367–1369) |
| 10:23 Let us maintain unmoved the profession of hope. . . . | Trust (1059, 1074) |
| 10:24 Let us consider each other. . . . | Works of mercy (742) |
| 10:25 Let us not desert our gathering. . . . | Mass attendance (914, 1584)<br>Desire for Eucharist (641, 832). |
| 12:1 Let us throw off all encumbrances. . . .<br>Let us run our course. . . . | Desire for God (807, 1771, 1826, 1820)<br>God's will be done (374, 1264, 1667, 1740) |
| 12:2 Let us gaze on Jesus. . . . | Look to Jesus (177, 527, 561, 1663) |
| 12:12–13 Let us strengthen our hands and knees, and make a straight path. | Take refuge in the Merciful Heart (801, 1033, 1287, 1348, 1621, 1629)<br>Holy Communion (704) |

| 13:13 Let us go outside the camp, hearing his insult. | Oblation (136, 1680) |
|---|---|
| 13:15 Let us offer up a sacrifice of praise. . . . | Offering as holocaust (1680, 1826) |
| 13:17 Obey your leaders and be submissive. | Obedience (354, 624, 645, 910) |
| 13:18 Pray for us. | Prayer for leader (202, 925, 953, 1348) |

C. Diary of Blessed Faustina Compared with the Letter
   to the Hebrews.

Symbols:

( ) *Special Urgency of Mercy*, Franciscan University Press,
   Steubenville, Ohio; Marian Helpers, Stockbridge,
   Massachusetts.

[ ] *Now Is the Time for Mercy*, Franciscan University
   Press; Marian Helpers.

(D.) *Divine Mercy in my Soul: The Diary of the Servant of
   God Sister M. Faustina Kowalska*, Marian Helpers,
   Stockbridge, Massachusetts.

| DIARY OF BLESSED FAUSTINA | LETTER TO THE HEBREWS |
|---|---|
| God is MERCIFUL (6) [I. 1–2] | 4:15–5:10 |
| Trust God (5) [I. 2–3] | 3:1–4:14; 11:1–12:13 |
| Only source of peace/ salvation (6, 7) (D. 300) | 9:28; 10:1–18 |
| Be merciful (7) [I. 4] | 12:14–13:18 |
| Glorify His mercy (5) (D. 300) | 13:15; 13:21 |
| Special vessels of mercy: Feast (8) [II. 5] Novena (8) [II. 6] Chaplet (8) [II. 4] | 4:15–16; 9:27–28 13:15, 18 5:7; 9:27–28; 10:10 |

| | |
|---|---|
| Image (8) [II. 3]<br>    Rays<br>    Blood & water<br>    White robe | 9:14, 28<br>1:3<br>9:14<br>2:17; 5:9-10; 7:1-28 |
| Interceding for mercy<br>    [III. 2] | 4:15–16; 5:7; 7:25; 12:23;<br>    13:15, 18 |
| Spiritual life of Blessed<br>    Faustina<br>    Humble obedience to<br>    the will of God<br>    Mary (9) | 5:8; 10:4–10<br>11:11–12:13 |
| Victims:<br>    Suffering with Christ<br>    (II) [III. 1] | 9:14; 10:10; 13:12–16 |
| Priest:<br>    Eucharist-offering<br>    (12) [III. 1] (D. 684,<br>    757, 832) | 9:14; 10:10; 13:12–16 |
| Merciful Heart (1) [III. 3] | 8:10; 10:15–18;<br>Jer 18:11–12; Ezek 36:26 |
| Jesus is High Priest (D.<br>    684, 757, 832) | 2:17; 5:9–10; 7:1–28 |
| Jesus is coming again (1)<br>    [III. 3] | 9:28; 10:25 |
| Urgency (1, 2) [Introduc-<br>    tion] | 2:1–4; 5:11–6:12 |

# APPENDIX B

## Divine Mercy: The Fulfillment
## of the Pentecostal Renewal

Along with others, I have watched the Catholic charismatic renewal undergo many changes. I have asked myself such questions as: "What Happened? What was missing? Where did it go off the track?" Some persons have responded to these questions with exhortations to "renew the renewal" by stirring up the gifts of the Holy Spirit and fanning into flame the fire of the Holy Spirit, and all with good intentions.

These attempts to rekindle the fire of the Holy Spirit are not adequate unless we know the goal of the charismatic renewal. Why are we fanning the flame? We need to start with a return to the first name used to describe the renewal, a *pentecostal renewal*, in order to have a fuller understanding of the goal. The goal is not just a charismatic renewal, a renewal of the gifts of the Holy Spirit, but rather, the goal is a renewal *by* the Holy Spirit Himself. The goal is a new Pentecost.

We need something that has been missing all these years in order to achieve the goal of a new Pentecost. Gradually, in my twenty-four years of involvement with the renewal, I have come to recognize and understand more fully just what this missing element is. As I have written earlier in this book, it was early in the morning on the Feast of All Saints, November 1, 1968, that I experienced a quickening of the Holy Spirit in my whole being. I was kneeling before the Blessed Sacrament at

Assumption University in Windsor, Ontario, a few hours after a group of students had prayed with me in Ann Arbor for the Baptism of the Holy Spirit. The experience of being quickened by the Holy Spirit was a very special moment for me because I was in the midst of a prolonged depression and deep anxiety over the post-Vatican II Church. I heard within my heart the words, "Now, can you tell my people of my compassion and love?"

At this moment, I am very aware that the word on my heart twenty-five years ago was a commission to proclaim the compassionate love of God, His Divine Mercy. That moment before the Blessed Sacrament was a major turning point in my life. I was drawn so deeply into the life and work of the Holy Spirit that I was encouraged to resign a professorship at the University of Windsor, to set aside sixteen years of teaching and research in biochemistry, and set out on a pilgrim's journey of full time renewal work with priests. For the next sixteen years, I ministered to thousands of priests at retreats in four continents and at a house of intercessory prayer for priests.

The pilgrimage continued with the team of the Fraternity of Priests, to be followed by still another transition, a time of solitude. I was challenged to go into solitude to "seek the Lord alone. Alone!" For the better part of a year, I did just that, and it was in solitude that I again heard the call, "Proclaim My mercy."

Based upon a growing sense of the urgent need in the Church and the world for Divine Mercy, I have tried to proclaim God's mercy. The more time I spend before the Blessed Sacrament, the more I am challenged to trust the Lord. I have been encouraged to spend three hours a day before the Blessed Sacrament as a plea for the whole world. Only now am I beginning to realize the challenge of November 1, 1968, "Proclaim My mercy."

It is out of the experience of solitude and out of the three hours daily prayer base that I look at the charismatic renewal of the Church. I have experienced sorrow over the situation in prayer groups and covenant communities in this country. I was so much a part of them in Ann Arbor and Steubenville. Their committed life style was a challenge to me and a living example in my teachings and writings over the years.

What is the missing element in the charismatic renewal? Divine Mercy?1 I have considered various aspects and dimensions of the renewal and found that Divine Mercy is the essential element in every one of them. Without Divine Mercy there is distortion, a caricature of what God intends. With Divine Mercy, the Spirit of Love is poured out of the pierced Heart of Jesus and into our hearts (cf. Rom 5:1-5), and God's plan to have mercy on all is fulfilled (cf. Rom 11:32).

The text of Sacred Scripture that for me related the work of the Holy Spirit to mercy is from Saint Paul's letter to Titus:

When the kindness and love of God, our Savior appeared, He saved us; not because of any righteous deeds we had done, but because of His mercy. He saved us by the renewal of the Holy Spirit. This Spirit He lavished on us through Jesus Christ our Savior, that we might be justified by His grace and become heirs, in hope of eternal life. You can depend on this to be true. [Titus 3:4-8.]

It is all gift. All grace. All mercy. All the work of the Holy Spirit! "And you can depend on this to be true." The Holy Spirit is the Spirit of Mercy poured into our hearts. Without Divine Mercy we have no renewal.

I have looked at many aspects of the charismatic renewal in the light of this relationship between the Holy Spirit and Divine Mercy. My list is open-ended; you can add to it with your own experience and extend the list beyond the twelve points I have considered.

## BAPTISM IN THE HOLY SPIRIT

Without Divine Mercy, without the love poured from the pierced Heart of Jesus, the baptism in the Holy Spirit is a baptism in power and therefore, one of control. It stops short of the Cross of Christ, and suffering has no meaning or value. With Divine Mercy, baptism in the Holy Spirit is also a baptism of blood, a "moving on" (Heb 6) to the pierced Heart of Jesus, which is the source of all mercy. The Holy Spirit convicts us of sin, that is, the world in us, in order to bring us to the source of all mercy, the Cross of Christ. There we are baptized in His mercy!

It is only when we are immersed in the Divine Mercy that we can carry out the command of Jesus to "be merciful even as your Father is merciful" (Luke :36). In mercy, suffering has meaning and value. The fulfillment of the baptism in the Holy Spirit is to be baptized in His mercy. This is the key to renewal, the fullness of the baptism of water, Spirit, and blood—and these three are one (cf. 1 John 5:8).

## PASTORAL CARE

Pastoral care is the key to Christian community. Without Divine Mercy, without compassionate love, pastoral care becomes "pastoral control." We have seen the devastating effects of this in some of the covenant communities. With Divine Mercy pastoral care becomes "pastoral love." This is the term used and the goal written of in various Vatican II documents (e.g., *Presbyterorum Ordinis* [*Decree on the Ministry and Life of Priests*]).

## THE WORD OF GOD

Sacred Scripture is central to the renewal, but without Divine Mercy, without faithful love, it becomes law and, "the Word becomes a book!" But with Divine Mercy, "the Word becomes flesh and dwells among us." The Word, born of Mary, continues to be present among us in His Church and in the Sacraments, and uniquely in the Holy Eucharist.

## FAITH

Without Divine Mercy, without the good works of mercy, faith becomes presumption and a form of angelism. With Divine Mercy faith becomes our salvation and sanctification. The good work is trust, a living faith in Jesus Christ, our Lord and Savior.

## GIFTS OF THE HOLY SPIRIT

The gifts of the Holy Spirit are key to the charismatic renewal of the Church, but without Divine Mercy, without love as Saint Paul wrote (cf. 1 Cor 13), they become a form of control and a power game. For example, healing gifts become a status symbol. With Divine Mercy, the gifts of the Holy Spirit are instruments of compassion and building community. Healing becomes a means of growing in holiness.

### PRAISE OF GOD

Exuberant praise without Divine Mercy, without a committed love, becomes an emotional high, or is empty, and is just a technique. With Divine Mercy, praise of God becomes a worship of the Living God.

### PROCLAMATION OF JESUS AS LORD

The proclamation of Jesus as Lord is the central reality of the Gospels and an integral part of the charismatic renewal. Without Divine Mercy, without life-giving love, however, this proclamation is not "good news" because it portrays God without the saving mercy poured out for us on Calvary. This can cause a feeling of control and bondage and evangelization is then a "know-it-all" imposition of partial truth. With Divine Mercy, the proclamation of Jesus Christ as Lord gives interior freedom to the children of God, bringing us out of the slavery of sin. Evangelization is then received as the Good News.

### REPENTANCE AND CONVERSION

Repentance and conversion are the very message of Jesus, but without Divine Mercy, without forgiving love, they keep us as the elder son of the parable of the prodigal son (cf. Luke 15) and the Pharisee who prays in the temple with head unbowed (cf. Luke 18:9-14), with no mercy nor justification, but rather with condemnation. With Divine Mercy we experience forgiveness, peace, and joy. Moreover, with Divine Mercy we can forgive others and be reconciled to God and one another.

## KNOWLEDGE

It is important that we know the truth because the truth will set us free (cf. John 8:32). Without Divine Mercy, without a love rooted in truth, however, knowledge becomes pride, power and control. With Divine Mercy, knowledge is truth; it is humility.

## THE CHURCH

The Mystical Body of Christ, the Church, without Divine Mercy, without covenant love, becomes a human organization with all its sins and weaknesses. With Divine Mercy the Church is the human-divine organism. It is the mystery of Christ in you (cf. Col 1:27-28). It is the covenant of the family of God.

## EUCHARIST

The Eucharist is a very sensitive issue in our time. Even Saint Paul in his time had to deal with it. Without the recognition that the consecrated bread and wine are the Body and Blood of the Lord, as the humble presence of Mercy itself, and the recognition of the assembly gathered in the obedience of faith under our shepherds, we continue to be sick and dying as Saint Paul describes in First

Corinthians 11:17-34. But with the recognition of the Eucharist as the miracle of mercy, we fulfill the teaching of Vatican II which calls the Eucharist the "summit and source" of the Church's life. Then we recognize the Eucharist as a miracle of mercy, the presence of Mercy itself, the sacrifice of Mercy, and a communion of Merciful Love.

## ECUMENISM

Ecumenism is at the origins of the pentecostal renewal. Without Divine Mercy, without truth and forgiving love it is not ecumenism, but a non-denominationalism, or better, the lowest common denominator type of relationship. But with *Mercy* we share all our Catholic treasures of the redemptive incarnation and the truth of the mediated grace of Sacraments, culminating in the Eucharist, as mercy present. We share the mediated intercession of saints, with Mary, our Queen Mother, and we share the mediated authority given to Peter.

## MARY

Without Divine Mercy, without tender and life-giving love, there is no mother, just an abstraction—if not a distraction to some Christians. Without Mary there is no Jesus, and no renewal. With Divine Mercy, Mary is Mother of Mercy, the Mother of Jesus, the Mother of God, the Mother of the Church, and our Merciful Mother dispensing the Lord's mercy to us in need. She is the spouse of the Holy Spirit and she is the Mother of the New Pentecost. As Father Harold Cohen, S.J., states it:

In my opinion, the Charismatic Renewal will not achieve the full purpose God has for it until Mary comes into her rightful place with the leaders and people of the Charismatic Renewal. And, in my opinion, the Marian movement will not achieve the full purpose God has for it until the people open up to the fullness of the Holy Spirit, the baptism in the Holy Spirit.

What happened with the Apostles and disciples at that first Pentecost in the Upper Room must happen again today. United in heart and mind and together with Mary, the Mother of the Church, Peter and the disciples called down the Holy Spirit. We need to unite around Peter and Mary and cry out for the fullness of the Holy Spirit "to renew the face of the earth."

This was the prayer of Pope John XXIII for the Second Vatican Council. He prayed that the Kingdom of God would come to fulfillment. The Latin word he used was *amplificet*, and it means to bring to fulfillment, to bring to the top of a vessel and overflow.

We need the overflow of the Holy Spirit, the Spirit of Mercy, God's love poured through the pierced Heart of Jesus, flowing into our hearts and overflowing with Divine Mercy to all in need.

This is the mission of Jesus, and of His Church, to make mercy present. "To make mercy present" is the summary of the encyclical of Pope John Paul II *Dives in Misericordia* and a key concept in *Redemptor Hominis.*

"To make mercy present" is to fulfill the Lord's command, "Be merciful even as your Father is merciful" (Luke 6:36).

"To make mercy present" is the fulfillment of the pentecostal renewal of the Church, a new Pentecost!

"To make mercy present" is the fulfillment of the plan of God, to have mercy on all (cf. Rom 11:32).

Let us turn to Mary, our Merciful Mother, and to the Holy Spirit, who united together, gave us Jesus—MERCY PRESENT!

---

[1]Divine Mercy is the second name for love (Pope John Paul II, *Dives in Misericordia*). Divine Mercy is God's love poured out: the Father's love poured out in creating us, the Son's love poured out in redeeming us, and the Holy Spirit's love poured out in sanctifying us.